CHILD ABUSE:
Intervention and Treatment

Edited by

Nancy B. Ebeling, MSSA, ACSW
District Executive, Children's Protective Services, Massachusetts Society for the Prevention of Cruelty to Children, Boston, Massachusetts
Treasurer, Children's Advocates, Inc., Boston, Massachusetts

Deborah A. Hill, MSW
Caseworker, Casework Consultant, Trauma Team Coordinator, Children's Social Service Department, Massachusetts General Hospital, Boston, Massachusetts
President, Children's Advocates, Inc., Boston, Massachusetts

PSG PUBLISHING COMPANY, INC.
Littleton, Massachusetts

4th Printing, 1979

Printed in the United States of America.

International Standard Book Number: 0-88416-026-2

Library of Congress Catalog Card Number: 74-82430

AUTHORS

Paul D'Agostino, MSW
formerly Supervisor with Inflicted Injury
Unit
Department of Public Welfare

Ann L. Arvanian, ACSW
Senior Social Worker, Boston and
Greater Boston Office
Children's Protective Services of
M.S.P.C.C.

Nancy C. Avery, ACSW
Supervisor, Boston and Greater Boston
Office
Children's Protective Services of
M.S.P.C.C.

Shirley L. Bean, ACSW
Project Coordinator for the Parents Center Project for the Study and Prevention of Child Abuse
Parents and Children's Services

Nancy B. Ebeling, ACSW
District Executive, Boston and Greater
Boston Office
Children's Protective Services of
M.S.P.C.C.

Shirl E. Fay, ACSW
Supervisor, Boston and Greater Boston
Office
Children's Protective Services of
M.S.P.C.C.

Leslie Gardner, MEd
Director, Gilday Center

Gail Garinger, Attorney
Children's Hospital Medical Center

Andrew D. Guthrie, Jr., MD
Executive Director, Bunker Hill Health
Center of the Massachusetts General
Hospital
Assistant Professor of Pediatrics,
Harvard Medical School

Gerald Hass, MD
Physician in Chief, South End Community Health Center

Associate Clinical Professor of Pediatrics,
Boston University School of Medicine
Clinical Instructor in Pediatrics, Harvard
Medical School

Deborah A. Hill, MSW
Caseworker, Trauma Team Coordinator
Children's Social Service
Massachusetts General Hospital

James N. Hyde
Administrator, Family Development
Study
Children's Hospital Medical Center

Irving Kaufman, MD
Child and Adult Psychoanalyst
Consultant to Children's Protective Ser-
vices, Boston Children's Services, Al-
bany Jewish Family and Children's
Service, and Polaroid Corporation
Faculty, Harvard Medical School and
Smith College School of Social Work

Joanne D. Lipner, ACSW
Casework Supervisor
New England Home for Little Wanderers
(formerly associated with Inflicted Injuries Department of Public Welfare)

Alan N. Marks, MD
Director, In-Patient Psychiatric Services
for Children
Tufts New England Medical Center
Assistant Professor of Psychiatry and
Pediatrics
Tufts University School of Medicine

Elizabeth H. McAnulty, RN
Public Health Nurse
Trauma X Team
Children's Hospital Medical Center

Anne E. McDonald, ACSW
Medical Social Worker
Department of Pediatrics
Boston City Hospital

Eli H. Newberger, MD
Director, Family Development Study

iii

Children's Hospital Medical Center
Instructor in Pediatrics, Harvard Medical
School

Arthur H. Rosenberg, LLM, JD
Faculty, Harvard Medical School, Department of Psychiatry
Legal Consultant for McLean Hospital and Jewish Family and Children's Service of Boston

Mildred Salins Sinofsky, MSW
Supervisor of Social Service
Department of Public Welfare, Family

and Children's Service, Inflicted Injury Unit
Coordinating Social Worker, Gilday Center

Cassie L. Starkweather
Organizer, Boston Chapter of Parents Anonymous

S. Michael Turner, ACSW
Director of Social Work
Parents and Children's Services
Advisor, Boston Chapter of Parents Anonymous

TABLE OF CONTENTS

PREFACE

This book is a compilation of papers selected from those given at the 1972 and 1974 Children's Advocates, Inc. New England Child Abuse Symposia. Additionally, material was written specifically for the book. The papers represent the thinking and experience of people from the medical, psychiatric, social work, legal, and lay communities. They describe a positive approach to the problem, viewing child abuse as a symptom of serious family problems, meriting careful and thorough evaluation and treatment. From both the individual and multidisciplinary points of view they illustrate various therapeutic methods which have proved helpful in working with families. Also included in the book are discussions of resources and programs for parents and professionals which may enhance family functioning.

The authors, professionals from various disciplines involved directly in dealing with child abuse and neglect, have detailed their philosophies and experiences. While the authors share a common philosophy, the diversity of programs and varying methods and approaches to the subject provide the reader of any discipline, setting, or geographical area with an opportunity to make use of something applicable to his own specific needs.

ACKNOWLEDGEMENTS

Children's Advocates, Inc. is grateful to the people connected with the Boston Globe, whose spirit of public concern and willingness to help greatly encouraged us. We are appreciative of the special interest directly shown by Davis Taylor, Publisher, and John I. Taylor, President. The Boston Globe granted funding for both symposia and helped to educate the public as to the complexities of the problems of child abuse and neglect through the sensitive press coverage and personal interest of Herbert Black, Senior Medical Writer, and Jean Dictz, Social Science Editor. We thank the other two sponsors of the November, 1972 symposium: the Massachusetts Department of Public Welfare—Division of Family and Children's Services provided personnel time and help with mailing, and the Boston University School of Social Work provided space for the symposium.

Our co-sponsors for the January, 1974 symposium were the Boston Globe, the Junior League of Boston, Inc., whose enthusiastic volunteers provided the willing and capable hands for the arrangements, and Harvard-Radcliffe University, whose commitment to continuing education was demonstrated by providing facilities and services for the symposium.

The symposium committee of Children's Advocates was responsible for the planning and the presentation of the two symposia. Those Children's Advocates members who served on the 1972 committee were: Deborah Hill, Chairman, Massachusetts General Hospital; Marianne Boltz, St. Margaret's Hospital; Elizabeth Colligan, Children's Hospital Medical Center; Nancy Condit, Junior League; Paul D'Agostino, Department of Public Welfare; Evelyn DeMille, New England Medical Center Hospital; Nancy Ebeling, Children's Protective Services; Marilyn Feinberg, volunteer, Department of Public Welfare; Dr. Andrew Guthrie, Jr., Massachusetts General Hospital; John Hagenbuch, Jr., Department of Public Welfare; Elsa-Ruth Herron, St. Elizabeth Hospital; Nancy Hoit, Junior League; Elaine Jacobson, Middlesex County Juvenile Probation Office.

The 1974 symposium committee members were: Nancy Ebeling, Children's Protective Services, and Marianne Boltz, St. Margaret's Hospital—co-chairmen: Evelyn DeMille, New England Medical Center Hospital; Marilyn Feinberg, volunteer, Department of Public Welfare; Deborah Hill, Massachusetts General Hospital; Joanne Lipner, Department of Public Welfare; Sharon Ossenbruggen, Junior League; Nancy Poor, Junior League; Jean Yozell, Family Counseling Service.

Finally, we acknowledge with special thanks all of the speakers who participated in the two symposia and those who so generously contributed their papers to this book. We thank them and the many others who gave freely of their time and energy toward the success of these symposia.

All proceeds from the sale of this book will go toward the work of Children's Advocates, Inc.

Membership, Children's Advocates, Inc.

Boston Children's Services
Boston City Hospital
Boston Juvenile Court
Cambridge City Hospital
Carney Hospital
Children's Hospital Medical Center
Children's Protective Services
Division of Family and Children's Services
Department of Public Welfare—Assistance Payments
Department of Public Welfare—Volunteer Department
Family Counseling Service—Region West
Junior League of Boston, Inc.
Middlesex County Juvenile Probation Office
Malden Hospital
Massachusetts General Hospital
North Shore Children's Hospital
Parent's and Children's Services
Roxbury Comprehensive Community Health Center
South Boston Community Health Center
St. Elizabeth Hospital
St. Margaret's Hospital
Shriners Hospital—Burns Institute
South End Community Health Center
Tufts New England Medical Center

INTRODUCTION

In response to the increasing demand for knowledge and the growing need for education in the areas of child abuse and neglect, Children's Advocates, Inc., an interdisciplinary committee on child abuse and neglect in the Greater Boston Area, held two symposia at which many of the papers which follow were presented. The writing of this text is in response to a growing awareness and interest on the part of the professional and lay communities to the complexity of the problem of child abuse and neglect. Professionals and nonprofessionals have come to realize that the problems of child abuse and neglect are not the exclusive problems of any one agency or the total responsibility of one profession. The entire community must share in this responsibility, and, as this is recognized, more people are searching for a direction in their efforts to service children and families.

What are people like who abuse their children? Who are they? Where are they? What kind of person will the battered child grow up to be? Experience and research in this area have enabled us to spot some common characteristics in the abusing and/or neglectful parent. In the majority of cases we see an individual who cares about his or her child and wants to be a good parent, except that this individual is handicapped by an emotionally deprived and harsh background, commonly characterized by abuse or neglect. With varying degrees, we see a disturbed, overwhelmed, sometimes isolated individual with little confidence or self-esteem, looking as a last resort to his child to meet his needs. Parenting is learned. The battered and neglected child of today may become the battering and neglecting parent of tomorrow.

Studies show child abuse and neglect to transcend all socio-economic groups. The number of childhood injuries, deaths, and instances of deprivation is phenomenal. The number of parents who suffer anguish in relation to these same problems is greater still.

In what ways do parents who have potential for abusing their children present their concerns? How can professionals learn to recognize early pleas for help? In the papers which follow, the authors will describe the various ways parents ask for help. Experience shows that many families in trouble respond with clear relief inwardly, if not outwardly, when someone finally directly and honestly confronts them with what is happening and offers them help. This awareness of external controls may actually be welcomed, particularly to the parent who feels helplessly out of control. It is our failure to recognize this which often permits the pattern of minor injuries or incidents to go on until it is too late to salvage a child and family from a permanently damaging injury or experience.

Hope for the future clearly lies in the early detection and prevention of child abuse and neglect.

What kinds of services help these families? All papers in this text reflect the philosophy which Children's Advocates, Inc. espouses— namely, that child abuse and neglect are *symptoms* of serious family unhappiness or dysfunctioning and that successful intervention involves treatment of the entire family unit toward alleviation of the stresses which resulted in the symptom. Keeping families together and strengthening family life is a primary goal. If, after careful and thoughtful evaluation, the child's safety cannot be provided for in his or her own home, placement outside the home is necessary. We see the use of the courts in this instance as positive and highly therapeutic. The ultimate goal is the return of the child to his or her home as soon as care and protection can be assured. Every child has a right to a sense of permanency and a feeling of belonging. It is crucial, therefore, that decisions pertaining to the child's future be given utmost priority, so that he or she can be provided with the opportunity to establish and maintain lasting relationships. In like manner, parents who cannot give adequate parenting should be helped to be relieved of this responsibility and to be freed from destructive relationships which are not amenable to change.

A second conviction members of Children's Advocates share is that the prevention and treatment of child abuse requires the energies of a variety of disciplines working together in a thoughtful, helpful, unified approach. Families with such sizable problems require services from many fields—social service, medicine, law and education, to name some.

Whose responsibility is this problem? Because of the number of families in need of help and the amount of help they need, it is apparent that no single agency or institution can be totally responsible for the needs of these families. There has been a tendency on the part of nonprotective agencies to avoid treatment of this problem, primarily, we think, out of lack of knowledge and insight as to the needs of these families. Indeed, the community physician, agency, or hospital is in the best position to provide early detection and therapeutic intervention in families where child abuse or neglect might be prevented. We would suggest that the community share heavily in the responsibility and opportunity to intervene decisively in these families, working in conjunction with whatever state agency is legally responsible for the treatment of vulnerable children and their families.

The professional who refers families to another community resource should first look at what he or she hoped the resource could do that he or she could not. What were the expectations? Could the other agency realistically provide a service that he or she could not, or was he or she seeking the miracle cure we all sometimes wish we had? In the extreme case, at the time of referral, was a child in such jeopardy that what was really needed was a request to the court to intervene rather than the protective agency. While increasing numbers of physicians, agencies, and hospitals have exercised their responsibility to take protective action for their own clients, there still exists a need to help others see and accept their responsibility and then act appropriately.

What are the feelings and attitudes of the professionals who deal with this problem? How can they be helped to recognize and deal with their feelings? The emotionally charged nature of the problem evokes strong feelings in us all. Some may feel a sense of outrage; others feel helpless. In others, the ambivalence reflecting both the wish to punish and the need to rescue may cause an individual to overreact on the one hand, or, on the other hand, to become immobilized. While concern about child abuse has grown rapidly, understanding and knowledge of the problem have not always kept pace. Lack of understanding and subjective attitudes may often stand as barriers to the development of good community programs. In the papers which follow, much attention is directed to this crucial area, as the success of intervention and treatment is directly related to the feelings and attitudes of the helping person.

How can professionals of different agencies be helped to deliver coordinated, well-planned, and helpful services to families? How can professionals and agencies work together to develop new service programs? The thread which ties all of the authors or their agencies together is Children's Advocates, Inc. Chapter 24 describes how this interdisciplinary group formed and developed and how it has provided the nucleus from which much of the impetus and energy for program development has come.

The chapters which follow guide the reader through the complicated problems of casefinding, diagnosis of needs, and the process of recognizing and dealing with the attitudes and feelings which can arise. Authors also address themselves to the crucial aspects of communication, management, and treatment.

Although all of the authors practice in urban areas, we believe that the basic philosophies, theories, and principals described can be applied to any area—urban, suburban, or rural.

We hope it will be useful in helping the reader think through the complexities of the problem, in helping shape his or her attitudes, and in providing a guide for the kind of program development which we in Children's Advocates, Inc. have found helpful and satisfying. Hope for the future lies in recognition of the early signs of abuse and neglect and in the conviction that each one of us shares in the challenge of a total community effort toward prevention and treatment.

Nancy B. Ebeling, MSSA, ACSW
Deborah A. Hill, MSW

PART ONE

A THERAPEUTIC
APPROACH

1 Thoughts on Intervention

Nancy B. Ebeling, ACSW

In two days of general meetings and workshops, Children's Advocates does not intend to give a prescription for a fool-proof or infallible solution to the very complex and frequently misunderstood problem of child abuse. We do hope, however, that the symposium will give you fresh ideas and reinforce and crystalize your thinking. For those of you who have had a lot of experience in protective service, we hope it will strengthen your convictions and have a reconstituting effect.

This chapter discusses some thoughts on intervention from the point of view of the community and then, more specifically, some ingredients important to beginning intervention into family situations where children are at risk.

Let us look first at the word "intervention." It is a word that has frequent usage in today's vocabulary, on the national and international scene, in our local communities, and particularly in human services. To relate it more directly to our work with people: we hear and use such phrases as community intervention, agency intervention, intervention techniques, intervention approaches, etc. *The American Heritage Dictionary* gives several definitions of intervention, among which are (1) to

3

enter or occur extraneously, or (2) when used in referring to nations, to interfere, usually through force or threat of force, and (3) to come in or between so as to hinder or modify. From a negative point of view, we can think of intervention as coming between, hindering, or interfering. This definition has a flavor of obtrusiveness, of forcing one's self or one's ideas on another, without invitation. From a positive view, however, we can think of intervention as entering a situation so as to modify—to help or to work with another person in altering a situation.

How we view intervention and our role in the process are important issues to consider if we are directly or indirectly involved in the protection of children at risk. Actually, protecting children at risk, in any setting, is basically a process of intervention which provides parents with an opportunity to change, to resolve, or to cope with the circumstances or problems which are contributing to their neglectful or abusive behavior toward their children.

Attitudes make a considerable difference in approaching a problem; in neglect and abuse situations, there is absolutely no question that community attitudes and professional individual attitudes provide a climate which can spell the difference between successful, unsuccessful, or mediocre service. This chapter will not attempt to delve deeply into the dynamics of community attitudes toward child abuse. However, some overall comments may prove helpful in understanding or clarifying where we are today, and why, with respect to community intervention.

Historically speaking, children have never been given very much consideration. Down through the ages, they have been maligned and mistreated, both physically and emotionally. As late as 1875, there were laws to protect animals but none to protect children from neglect or abuse. True, many charities cared for homeless, abandoned, or orphaned children—but not one law existed on the statutes to offer protection of the type given to animals. In 1875, the now famous case of Mary Ellen came to the fore. Mary Ellen, who was receiving cruel and abusive treatment from adults, had to be protected by the law used to protect animals.

Fortunately, the incident so aroused some citizens that a movement was begun to create private organizations to protect children known as "Societies for the Prevention of Cruelty to Children." The Massachusetts Society, the second such organization, was established in 1878 in Boston. It became a statewide private social agency which is now known as Children's Protective Services. While there has been considerable progress since 1875, it did take almost 90 years before legislation was passed which more specifically spelled out protection of children from abuse. The Battered Child Law was passed in 1964 in Massachusetts; similar laws now exist in all 50 states.

The point of this brief historical review is two-fold. First, it tells us that the still lingering reluctance of communities, both lay and professional, to recognize child abuse has a long-standing history; it is not just a product of today's world anymore than child abuse itself is. Second, the past can help put the present into perspective so that we can deal more effectively with the existing situation.

For many reasons communities have been reluctant to intervene on matters of child abuse, not only in terms of legislation but in regard to recognizing and dealing more directly with the problem itself. Certainly one factor in this reluctance is that parental rights have always taken precedence over the rights of children. It has always been thought that parents should have the right to raise their children without interference; this right also implied the right to impose discipline in whatever way they felt necessary. We would all certainly agree that families should not be subjected to external interference in normal circumstances; at the same time, neither can children be considered property or possessions. Only recently have the rights of children per se been seriously considered, studied, and watched over. In Massachusetts, for instance, organizations of recent origin set up for just these purposes include The Office for Children, Children's Lobby, and Children's Advocates, Inc.

Children's Advocates, Inc. is a good example of community intervention into child abuse. Its formation grew out of a desire on the part of individuals from various disciplines in the Boston community (1) to work together to provide a co-operative and co-ordinated approach to child abuse and then (2) to offer interpretation and education to others. Child abuse and neglect are not easy problems to deal with. It is essential that all health, education, and social welfare services keep their lines of communication open to each other in order to create a co-ordinated approach to intervention and treatment.

Another reason, I believe, for the reluctance on the part of the community to recognize child abuse is that recognition means having to deal with the problem and dealing with the problem means involvement and commitment—in this case, to a very serious and complex social problem. Child abuse itself is a problem which the public finds difficult to accept. Because it is an emotional subject, it arouses feelings—both positive and negative—and often produces a climate for biases, prejudices, and value judgments which can make responsible community intervention difficult. We know from long experience that most families who exhibit symptoms of abuse and neglect can and should be helped to become more adequate parents. Many individuals, however, have mixed feelings about child abuse; they are unclear about how to deal with it, so their reactions to parents are often punitive. Think of some of the dramatic and often hostile terminology used in describing parents—child beaters, child murderer, child abusers. A familiar misconception says that those who work with neglecting or abusive families have or should have some mysterious authority or magic wand to quickly remedy the situation by ordering parents to change or by removing a child or children immediately. This misconception causes conflicts; individuals who have such misconceptions sometimes are fearful of referring a family because of what they think might happen or, if they do refer, are upset when it does not happen.

Anyone who works in a protective service agency or who has responsibility for protective service or hospital trauma cases knows well the frustrations, pressures, and problems which occur in efforts to interpret and explain to people involved or interested in a family—people who may have biases and misinformation as well. Fortunately, there is a lessening of reluctance on the part of the community to recognize and diagnose child abuse; better provisions for prevention and intervention are beginning to be available. In the past few years, in fact, there has been a startling—though long overdue—increase in the amount of interest in protective services. As awareness of the problem grows, the desire for knowledge and understanding increases.

The success of direct intervention into families by individuals of helping professions depends on how we view our role and how we view the problem. Initial intervention into family situations where there may be neglect or abuse may vary in its approach, according to the setting in which we are working—an emergency room in a hospital, a neighborhood health center, a protective service social agency. However, some very basic similarities exist regardless of where the contact with a family is first initiated. First, how the initial interview is handled sets the stage, so to speak, for on-going work with parents; if mishandled, it may possibly end any hope for a continuing relationship. Second, it can provide us with some very important observations which can be helpful in developing a diagnostic assessment and then—if indicated—the beginning of a therapeutic plan.

It is important to emphasize at this point, however, that on some occasions, because of the serious pathology within a family and other circumstances beyond our control, no amount of skill will be sufficient to involve the family in a therapeutic plan. When this situation occurs, we may tend to chastise ourselves and be too self-critical. Such a response serves absolutely no good purpose; in fact, it is really self-defeating, for it can make us too subjective in our thinking and too vulnerable in other situations. We must be realistic in self-appraisal and in self-expectations when working with others. We do the best we can; we listen; we learn; we develop our skills; and we work at being in fine tune with our emotions—but we cannot expect the impossible of ourselves or others. If we do, we are seeking to bestow on ourselves higher powers than we are intended to have.

Child abuse and neglect are not easy problems to work with, but the field is stimulating and rewarding; it provides a challenge in understanding not only the problem but our reactions to it.

Let's look briefly at the families to whom we will be offering help. What are the general characteristics of abusive and neglecting parents? From a socio-economic standpoint, no typical family actually exists, since parents who are abusive or neglectful are from a cross section of the country. They are poor, middle income, wealthy, black, brown, or white. They may be lawyers, policemen, teachers, housewives, doctors, store clerks, electricians, mechanics, nurses, salesmen, or unemployed. They may live in rural, urban, or suburban areas.

Regardless of a family's sociological, cultural, or economic background, some characteristics are similar. The most common of these is severe emotional deprivation suffered by parents in their own growing up. Unfulfilled, very basic emotional needs of their own make it difficult, if not impossible, for parents to give to their children. They are in varying degrees isolated and are generally anxious and frightened in their role as parents. They become overwhelmed with the demands made on them by society and their children; they just cannot cope.

All of us who work with such troubled families know that both neglect and abuse are self-perpetuating. Parents who mistreat their children were once children themselves who were generally mistreated emotionally or physically by their own parents. They were made to feel inadequate and worthless; they certainly were never given any reason to trust or to love. Indeed, anyone growing up in such an environment cannot help but be distrustful and angry; in most instances, he or she will feel hate rather than love.

Dr. Fritz Redl, in his book *Children Who Hate,* very aptly describes this principle when he states:

> The children who hate, we must remember, are the children of neglect. They have been chronically traumatized, through repetitive frustrations of many of their basic needs. Indeed, we might speculate that they suffer from a disease entity directly stemming from neglect itself which might be called "neglect edema." Their frustration swells and festers, as it were, until even frustration, which is minor and painless, in terms of the "normal," becomes for them an intolerable challenge to control which they cannot meet. For each frustration, no matter how small the issue may be, is lumped together with the frustrations out of the past.[1]

---

1. Redl, F., and Wineman, D. *Children Who Hate.* Glencoe, Ill.: The Free Press, 1952.

All of us who work in protective services, regardless of the setting, realize from our experience that hostile and angry feelings are often used to hide the feelings of a frightened and anxious person. The parents we see already feel terribly inadequate; to tell them of our concern about the care of their children provokes additional feeling, which often results in anger and defensiveness.

As mentioned earlier, one of the most important elements in dealing with the symptoms of child abuse in families is the ability to understand and to deal with our own attitudes and feelings toward the family. The way we deal with our emotions—and whether or not we maintain objectivity—plays a crucial part in being able to help these seriously troubled families. If we are to be helpful, we cannot indulge ourselves by acting upon angry feelings, natural as they might be, toward a parent for treatment of a child. Developing self-awareness and insight—and maintaining patience and self-discipline—can sometimes be difficult tasks, but very vital ones.

Subjectivity may well result in the breaking off of a relationship with a family or the inability to even begin any kind of therapeutic approach. The parent will, in all probability, retreat or run; thus the opportunity to protect a child by helping his family may well be lost.

In the chapter entitled "The Social Worker and the Family," by Helen Alexander, from the book *Helping the Battered Child and His Family,* by Dr. Kempe and Dr. Helfer, Mrs. Alexander states that:

> Beginning to establish a relationship with these families is often the most difficult phase. Our own intense feelings about abuse and more specifically the feelings about particular parents, and what they have done to their child, must be openly recognized. In attempts to cloak the anger, we may hide behind authority and a need to protect the child. Anger is a natural reaction and protection of the children essential but when mixed together they can be explosive and lethal to the development of any therapeutic approach with the family.[2]

When we are dealing with such emotionally charged problems, which so specifically relate to the parent-child relationship, it is possible that various internal reactions may occur which can hinder our ability to help. These reactions can take various forms such as over-identification with a child, misuse of authority, anger toward a parent, over-protectiveness toward a child, and a need to rescue, especially when working with very emotionally needy and crisis-ridden families.

---

2. Alexander, H. The Social Worker and the Family. Edited by C. H. Kempe and R. E. Helfer. In *Helping the Battered Child and His Family.* Philadelphia: Lippincott, 1972.

In summary, let me re-emphasize our commitment that most parents with problems of child abuse and neglect can be helped. Each family must be individualized and treated with empathy and with respect for individual differences. The attitudes of social workers, physicians, nurses, teachers, school counselors, and others are quickly perceived by parents and responded to accordingly. Successful community intervention into problems of child abuse depends greatly on community attitudes, just as successful individual intervention into family situations depends on our own attitudes and reactions.

PART TWO

CASEFINDING

2 Child Abuse, the Community, and the Neighborhood Health Center

Gerald Hass, MD

Child abuse most often occurs in the home; it should be considered a family and community problem. We know that the home may be rich or poor and that the community may be urban, suburban, or rural. This discussion concerns people of the inner city of Boston but it should not be interpreted to mean that the inner city is the only place where children are injured or neglected. We know that this is not the case.

In the inner city, the Neighborhood Health Center is intimately involved with—and in many respects has become the "family physician" to—the community it serves. The Health Center is probably better able to handle the medico-social diseases of the multi-problem family than any other provider in the community. The Health Center has on its staff community people who know what is going on in the community and who are in a position to do something to help families in crisis.

The two antennae of the Health Center are the receptionist and the outreach worker. The receptionist's job is to act pleasant, greet patients, and make them feel comfortable. She should not be regarded as a Health Professional; because of this, she is the least threatening person to patients. Patients confide more to her than they do to nurses and certainly more than they do to doctors. The receptionist might almost be called the "inreach worker."

An outreach worker travels out in the neighborhood, has a network of contacts, and, through work in facilitating patient care, provides friendly, supportive, and non-threatening practical services outside the Health Center. In a private practice setting, the outreach worker does not exist. Because the Neighborhood Health Center is situated where people live, it is well placed to be the most effective early warning system for identification and subsequent intervention in socio-medical problems. In retrospective examination of tragedies that we have all seen on hospital emergency floors, it becomes painfully obvious that many problems were predictable and that cries for help from families were not heard or, if heard, not understood.

We are all familiar with the mother who brings her child to the hospital with many complaints such as "he's always crying," "he has high fevers," or "he won't eat." When examination reveals no disease process the diagnosis is made of "well child," "anxious mother," and the treatment prescribed is "reassurance."

Unfortunately, after a series of these encounters, a physician's tolerance diminishes. He may become angry and send the mother and child away. The physician on the emergency floor is usually a junior house officer and, if he finds no abnormal signs, he does not seek help from a senior colleague who might look beyond the child—at the mother crying for help. It is very hard for many mothers (or fathers) to put into words their fears that they might injure their children. Instead, they often expect us to interpret and even sense their real feelings and concerns while they complain of more medically acceptable symptoms.

If prevention is our goal, then prediction should be one of the means to this end. Prediction depends upon information. The external or community grapevine provides continuous information for the Health Center staff to use but, unless the staff has an internal grapevine or the ability to communicate internally, little action will follow. The formal three-hour conference has no advantages over the day-to-day close and cooperative working relationship of Health Center colleagues who use short, task-oriented discussions to formulate and share the plans for intervention. In order to maximize time and effort in the busy hurley-burley workings of the Health Center, energies must be concentrated and applied where the need is the greatest. We therefore need to single out the patients of families who need the most care and the most time.

We should try to anticipate potential problems by identifying high-risk patients or patients in high-risk situations. It should be possible to identify a prenatal high-risk mother in social terms as well as in medical terms. Just as the obstetrician takes special precautions with a pregnant woman who has high blood pressure, sugar in her urine, a previous history of toxemia, or Rhesus sensitization, we should include the unwed teen-ager with an unwanted pregnancy, the pregnant mother who denies her pregnancy, and the mother who was herself abused as a child. Other identifying criteria may be applied in individual situations, depending on our judgement and on our knowledge of particular patients.

A general criterion which may be useful is trying to find out if the mother of a new baby is isolated from help—does she have a life line at a time of severe potential stress? The first few weeks with a crying baby can be a burden for any family even if they have family, social, and medical support. The isolated mother, who may also be severely depressed, may find these weeks intolerable. Without help or anticipatory guidance she may fall apart and present a high potential for child abuse or even infanticide.

Examples of high-risk categories are usually self-evident, but we should guard against falling into the trap of regarding poverty alone as a high risk, even though it may compound stresses placed on families. Other socio-medical problems such as drug abuse and alcoholism do not respect social class, and middle-class families may injure their children more often than we realize.

Some families may have multiple problems; yet they may be able to cope with them to an astonishing degree. We need to recognize this fact and concentrate our energies where the need is real.

We should look out for families where previous abuse or neglect has occurred, where a child is failing to thrive without apparent reason, where there are repeated minor injuries or ingestions, or where appointment keeping is extremely bad. A patient who does not show up repeatedly should be regarded as being a particularly high risk until we know that all is well—and that may only be determined by a home visit.

Having identified our high-risk patients, we need an internal system which helps us to share this information in a confidential way with the professional staff of the Health Center. Such sharing can be done by signifying in some acceptable way on the patient's chart that he or she is a risk. Some hospitals put a star on the chart and then stamp the inside cover with TRAUMA X in large type. Others suggest a numerical code on the front of the chart. In our Health Center, we have found using a red-covered record chart helpful because it stands out in the filing cabinet and requires no identifying names or diagnostic terms. Since we use different color charts for adults and children, another color seems to have escaped notice; it is not especially threatening to patients. It serves as a reminder for our staff to pay careful attention to the patients so identified. It is also easy to pull out 25 or 30 records and review progress in our patients from time to time. This review is an essential part of the process because all of us tend to repress our concerns about particularly difficult or unhappy problems. The problem-oriented chart is also a useful tool for reminding us of significant past and ongoing medical and social problems—if this method is used properly.

Having identified the problem patient, we need a plan for intervention. The plan should be as simple as possible and should be known and understood by the staff of the Health Center. The best plans go astray if some staff members are unaware of what the plan actually requires of them.

We must be prepared to take steps to confirm the diagnosis and remove the child if there is serious danger in the home. Such removal may mean arranging a speedy and smooth admission to the hospital. Mechanisms for handling high-priority referrals between Health Center and hospital are vital. It may be disasterous for a patient to be refused admission in the face of the concerns of the referring physician. Confirmation of the diagnosis in the hospital depends upon good history taking, clinical examination, x-rays, and documentation by photographs. Health Center staff should be prepared to work closely with hospital staff, attending case conferences and planning together. It is a sad fact that hospital admission remains one of the few immediate steps we can take to safeguard a child and help the family. A much more acceptable intervention might be a 24-hour crisis day care center to be used if the medical situation allows. Many hundreds of hospital days are used for custodial care because no other facility is available.

A knowledge of the mechanisms for referral to the state Division of Child Guardianship is essential. Workers from the Division will help to educate health professionals and work out their referral and intervention plans ahead of time. They will indicate methods of reporting and the legal requirements and provisions made to help families in crisis. It may be very helpful to contact the Division of Child Guardianship for guidance when the diagnosis is in question.

The final area that needs exploration is how to handle the family when a report of child abuse is being made. This raises the difficult and uncomfortable questions of who tells the family and how it should be done.

As a general rule, this notification is best done after the medical crisis is over; it is preferably done by the physician who will take responsibility in the hospital for care of the patient. It should be done in the presence of another person—either a social worker or nurse—and should be attempted as a measure of concern to help the family. It is, unfortunately, a very difficult thing to maintain this helping approach when it may be construed by the family as a punitive or threatening measure. Nevertheless, reassurance, support, and understanding will eventually succeed if these are offered in a helping spirit and if they produce tangible results.

3 Child Abuse: Early
Casefinding in a
Hospital Setting

Deborah A. Hill, MSW

The hospital social worker is in a position to deal with immediate
instances of child abuse. He or she can observe early warning signs and
thus offer a preventative approach to this problem.

This chapter discusses the social worker as casefinder, describes the
characteristics a social worker looks for to identify a potentially abusing
family, and illustrates these characteristics by case examples. It also
describes the use of a "vulnerable child list" in a hospital setting.

Child abuse is likely to occur when a parent (or caretaker)—with
the potential to be abusive to a child he or she perceives in a distorted
fashion as deserving of battering—experiences a crisis in daily life and
has no one except the child to turn to for help. The child is incapable
of meeting the parent's needs, so striking out at the child takes place.

The social worker can learn to recognize the characteristics in a
potential child abuser and, through offering early intervention and a
corrective treatment relationship, can identify what may constitute a
"crisis" for a given parent. The social worker can be the available "life
line" at this time of stress, and the crisis can be averted or made less
overwhelming by the presence of a trusted, helping person. This treat-

ment is difficult, occasionally impossible, to achieve with families who have little trust, and whose needs are great. However, when treatment is successful, child abuse can be prevented.

Treatment of child abuse is most successful when the abuse is viewed as a *symptom* of serious family dysfunctioning or unhappiness and when treatment addresses itself to the needs of both partners. In most situations, the active abuser is supported in his behavior by the partner, who passively condones the actions. It is unproductive and unhelpful for the social worker to seek answers as to "who did it." Rather, efforts are best directed toward determining whether or not abuse could likely have occurred in a given family and then toward treating the abuse as symptomatic of a total family problem. Every effort should be made to establish a helpful working relationship with the family, toward strengthening family life, and toward helping the parents view the child in a more positive way, so that the child's safe return home can be assured. In the majority of cases this course of action is possible. Where it is not, the involvement of the court in a positive way can be highly therapeutic. With more efforts directed toward early casefinding, families can be offered help on a preventative basis before rising pressures result in actual inflicted injuries.

Parents who abuse their children are people whose own dependency needs have not been met and whose early years were characterized by criticism from parents whose expectations they tried desperately to meet. These parents were often physically abused themselves. Abusing parents have markedly low self-esteem. They tend to find partners who abuse them and who cannot meet their needs.

The abusing parent is generally a socially isolated individual with little capacity to trust and reach out to people who could help. Experience has taught him or her that this course is not safe. This parent, then, is highly sensitive to demands and to feelings of failure or criticism. When these feelings become overwhelming, it is the child he or she looks to for comfort and support. When this is not forthcoming, abuse frequently takes place.

These parents have low tolerance for frustration, poor impulse control, and a sense of righteousness about discipline of their children. They may identify the child with what they see as the "bad" part of themselves.

The social worker may observe some of these characteristics in parents who visit the emergency wards, clinics, or inpatient services. In interviewing expectant mothers, social workers frequently hear a mother talk of an unwanted child who is perceived as a burden to her or who was fathered by someone who abandoned her or treated her badly. These mothers may already be identifying the unborn child in a negative way with themselves or someone else. The unborn child may be expected to fulfill a prescribed role in the parents' eyes—that is, to be a success in some area, or a solution to an unhappy marriage.

When a newborn baby is defective in some way, many feelings are aroused in parents who already feel so defective themselves. Illustrative of some of these issues is the case of a hospitalized newborn baby with a severe cleft palate; the case was referred to social service because the mother was not visiting the baby in the hospital and the doctor was concerned. When the worker talked with the mother, she learned of a highly vulnerable situation. The child was unwanted by his father. The father—in the course of arguments regarding this newborn—was physically abusing the mother. The mother had a history of attachments to abusive men. In a time of crisis in her past, she had terminated contact with two children of a previous marriage. The parents had not married because of their frictions. The mother could acknowledge to the worker that she, too, was concerned for the child's well-being in this situation but that she was unable to separate from the baby's father to provide safety for herself and the baby. The father was also seen, but he denied that there were any problems. This vulnerable situation necessitated the hospital's going to court to seek placement of the baby. The involvement of the authority of the court in a positive way resulted in the parents involving themselves productively in a treatment plan with the worker at the hospital. The successful outcome was the return home of the child.

The most important characteristic noted in parents with the potential to abuse is their inappropriate expectations of their children. One mother of a severely neglected, non-thriving infant was observed by her child welfare worker to say to her three-month-old girl, "you just lie there and I do all the work." This angry, depressed, frightened, unwed mother, in her attempts to hide the existence of the baby from her critical parents, was trying to deny her existence by providing minimal nurturance. The infant, when finally taken to the hospital, looked like a refugee.

A five-month-old boy was admitted to the hospital with bruising of the face in the form of a hand print. The mother of the infant, whose life experiences had taught her to please authorities and tell them what they want to hear, documented the history of abusive behavior on the husband's part. She, however, was totally unaware of her own involvement in undermining him and inciting him to anger. As time went on, we learned that the father, highly sensitive to his short stature and its implications for him of weakness, commonly roughhoused with his infant son. Clearly, he wanted his son to become the big, tough man he wished to be.

More common and subtle early signs of this "role reversal" may be observed by a social worker in his or her daily contacts with mothers and their small children. For example, a mother may expect her toddler to sit still while she talks, or she may seek and receive comfort from a child when she, herself, is in distress.

Abusing mothers have little confidence or trust that their own needs will be met. A fifteen-month-old boy was admitted to the hospital with a skull fracture. Through social service evaluation, we learned that a protective agency had been involved with the nineteen-year-old mother to help her mother her child. However, she had not been able to utilize this interest in herself. She had spent a lifetime caring for her ill mother. Just prior to the episode of trauma, she had lost the baby sitter on whom she had heavily relied. Further, the child had been viewed as defective because of an early and transitory episode of seizures. With the intervention of placement for the baby, this very needy mother was able to accept foster care and to make subsequent strides in self-esteem.

A sixteen-month-old child was admitted to the hospital; she subsequently died as a result of severe abdominal injuries sustained when she was kicked by her mother's abusive boyfriend. This mother had such low self-esteem that she selected abusive partners. She was so dependent on them that she, in effect, condoned their handling of her child.

Abusive parents often select a child whom they view as having their own "bad" characteristics and as therefore being deserving of battering. A mother presented herself in clinic with the verbalized concern that she was going to injure her three-year-old daughter. She perceived her daughter as "bad," willful, and stubborn like herself. Indeed, in response to the mother's expectations, the child had developed adult-like qualities of control. It was the child who controlled the mother and served as comforter. The child carried over this role to her nursery school group, where she mothered and bossed the other children. This mother had been subjected to much harshness, inconsistency, and little mothering as a child. She had selected an irresponsible, abusive husband, in keeping with her feelings of low self-worth. This mother was able to accept casework treatment for herself at the hospital; she was helped to refrain from injuring her children, despite their demands on her.

Unhappily, not all potentially abusive parents are able to ask for help directly. More often, parents' cries for help are very indirect. Mothers who repeatedly bring their children to one or to a variety of hospitals or clinics with seemingly minor complaints or with actually distorted impressions that a child is ill, are frequently asking for help—either in dealing with the child or in relief from the child.

The mother of a two-year-old boy presented herself in the Well Child Clinic; she was noted by the nurse to be unusually harried and anxious. Although the mother could not verbalize any problems, she used the time to talk about herself. She was observed to find the baby's normal demands on her quite frustrating. Therefore, the nurse scheduled the baby's innoculations in such a spaced manner that the mother could come regularly and slowly begin to establish trust in the nurse and in the hospital. Gradually, the mother could talk of her fears about leaving her abusive boyfriend and about how lonely she was. She was referred to social service, and more indications of her frustration with the child began to emerge. Factual material was clarified. Her age turned out to be sixteen rather than twenty-one. She later was able to call and ask for much needed temporary relief from the baby. She asked that the baby be hospitalized over the weekend. This request was accomplished; the mother visited daily and then took the baby home. Several days later the baby was seen in the emergency ward with bruised buttocks and was again admitted. This time the mother was tearfully able to accept placement.

The mother of a three-month-old infant repeatedly and frantically brought her baby to the emergency ward claiming he was having seizures and vomiting. She had recently been hospitalized for severe depression; she came from a deprived and rejecting background. She had temporarily placed the baby shortly after birth. She presented herself as hostile and expressed fear that the hospital staff would see her as an unfit mother and would want to place the baby—clearly a projection of her own wishes. The baby was ultimately hospitalized for observation of possible seizures; none were noted. Meanwhile, the mother had convinced the hospital staff to prescribe medication for seizures, which occurred by her history only. Continued medication would endanger the baby's health, and overdoses in themselves could cause seizures. Review of past and present history made it clear that the mother was really asking for relief from the care of the child in the only way she could. It was necessary for the hospital to request temporary placement through the courts.

Note should be made of vague, confusing, or contradictory reports given as to the cause of an injury. Parents who demonstrate unusual aggression in front of hospital personnel are, in their own way, asking for intervention from an external source, to provide the controls they lack from within. A mother who requests hospitalization of a child—for whatever reason—should be taken seriously. Often it is a warning sign that a mother has reached the limits of her endurance and needs relief from the care of the child. If, in addition to the mother's perception of the problem, the child is in reality a problem—for example, hyperactive or provocative—the chance is increased that abuse will take place. Because many of these frantic visits to the hospital may occur in emergency wards at odd hours of the night, it is important that attending house officers and nurses be made aware of the implications of these shrouded requests for help. They should learn to reach out to families, arranging for a return clinic visit when a social worker can meet them and help with some identified problem. If necessary, depending on the degree of tension in the mother-child relationship, the physician should admit the child to the hospital to provide a measure of relief and safety while the social worker evaluates the home situation.

An additional aid in casefinding is the use of a "vulnerable child list." This list names children who are felt by a concerned hospital or social agency to be vulnerable to abuse or severe neglect. Placement of a child's name and other identifying information on this list is, of course, done in a highly confidential manner. This information is made available to the cooperating agencies and hospitals on a regular routine basis as rapidly as possible. Abusing families in crisis tend to go to one institution after another in rapid succession.

Names of vulnerable children are kept in an available but confidential spot in hospital emergency rooms and clinics. When a member of a health team is concerned about a child, yet uncertain as to plan, often the confirmation that a child was previously felt to be vulnerable by another source helps in making a decision. It also helps the health team member coordinate a treatment plan.

In summary, potentially abusive parents present themselves in a variety of ways—hostilely denying problems, eager to please, verbally asking for help—with a variety of concerns about themselves or their children. Certainly, not all caretakers who have one or several of the common characteristics of abusing parents will decidedly batter their children. As noted, it takes the right ingredients of the potential to abuse, a child perceived as deserving of battering, a crisis for this family, and the lack of availability of help at that time. However, these are certainly families in need of treatment intervention; they are families to whom help can be offered on a preventative basis by social workers who have learned to recognize the early warning signs of families in distress.

4 Child Abuse on Main Street—Semantics in the Suburbs

Andrew D. Guthrie, Jr., MD

INTRODUCTION

A generation has passed since Caffey [1] described child abuse associated with subdural hematoma and multiple skeletal injuries. Various data (relating to incidence, vulnerability, psychopathology in the family, delineation of the nature of skeletal injuries, associated risk factors, specific profiles of abused and abuser) have accumulated since then. Gradually, the complexities of this family-centered illness are being recognized. In the past two decades, the existence of this phenomenon—that parents, caretakers, or adults in general can and do abuse children—has been accepted as fact. The intricacies of this disorder serve to emphasize the problems in formulating a system within the health care industry to identify, evaluate, and then individually manage each case currently known or suspected.

1. Caffey, J. Multiple fractures in the long bones of children suffering from chronic subdural hematoma. *Am. J. of Roentgenol:* 56: 163, 1946.

Neglect and abuse of children by parents and caretakers is known to occur in all socio-economic and ethnic groups in our society. In the recent reports relating to incidence and type of interventive programs available, this social illness is usually discussed in the context of urban, poor people. This selection is to be expected, since authors have gained their experiences and knowledge at urban-situated institutions such as medical schools, university-affiliated hospitals, and central offices of private and public social agencies. Such selection also explains the relatively high incidence of this "family disease process" reported in large cities, but it does not explain the relative dearth of cases reported from the suburbs. It is truly reflective of the double standards within the health system when an infant from a suburban address is admitted to a hospital as a "failure to thrive," while a similar infant from a neighborhood health center is transferred with a diagnosis of "question of neglect." Such differentiation may well represent a disservice to each infant.

Child abuse has been described as a multi-generationally determined family disease. It involves a scapegoat—an infant, a child, or an adolescent—who most frequently lives in an urban setting. The children who reside elsewhere are not being recognized and diagnosed as having problems relating to their rearing; specifically, child abuse is less visible in and is not being reported from the suburbs.

Several hypotheses are offered to explain this phenomenon:

1. A reluctance on the part of health-care providers to admit the existence of this disease.
   The nature of the professional training of physicians—with emphasis on the physical aspects of disease, diagnosis, and management—has contributed to disinterest in or disregard for the entire spectrum of bio-socially oriented health care. Ignorance of the content of the state mandatory reporting statute and of the mechanisms required for intervention is an additional burden for physicians. Anxiety regarding the legal implications of "being involved" by reporting a case of child neglect or abuse may not be lessened by the stronger language being incorporated into more recent reporting statutes; however, the punishment for not reporting becomes a greater burden.

2. Lack of coordination of services.
   The fragmentation into vertical service structures which is frequently noted in private practice of medicine in the suburbs interferes with an ability to communicate between the medical care arena and social agencies. The potential strengths of these vertical service connections should be extended into horizontal links among a variety of disciplines. Historically, social services have been regarded as essential only for the "poor." This practice establishes a bias

against any links that would increase the opportunity for social services to be involved in suburban communities. The bias is double-edged, since social agencies often see themselves as being needed solely—or more importantly—by urban poor. How much outreach effort is sought by or delivered to suburban populations?

3. Characteristics of "private" medical care.
   The characteristics of private medical care, other than those already considered, have an important bearing on the capacity or limitations for involvement in a family disease which is expressed as abuse or neglect of infants and children. The increasing numbers of specialists contribute to a partitioning of services to a family—services to children, to parents, or by organ system. The opportunity to assess a complaint or a problem within the context of the entire family is frequently lost. The tendency of the patient to offer a physical complaint as a means of gaining entrance into the care system also makes the task of uncovering the interpersonal or social problem more difficult. Finally, the relative accessibility of the physician in the suburban community—if not in person, then certainly by telephone—does afford a parent an opportunity to relieve the tensions provoked by crises in daily living. This circumstance provides symptomatic treatment initially, but it does not allow for an in-depth discussion of the basic problems which contribute to abusing or neglecting incidents.

THE BEST INTERESTS OF THE CHILD

A paradoxical situation exists for the physician who identifies himself as a family practitioner or primary caretaker when confronted by an infant or child with unexplained injuries in various stages of healing or by an infant who is failing to grow. It may appear necessary to arrive at a decision that will favor either the parents or the child. It is essential that the decision be made on the basis of causative factors, the vulnerability of the infant or child, and the needs of the parents or guardians.

The relatively small volume of reported cases of neglect and abuse from the private sector suggests that the integrity of the family takes precedence. Several states have addressed the issue of parents' rights versus the best interests of the child. The court is required to ensure that the parental right to custody yields to the child's best interests when these rights conflict.[2] In effect, the integrity of the family as a right of the parent must be considered secondary to what is in the best interests of the child, when abuse is the issue.

---

2. Breslin, R. F. *Seton Hall Law Review.* Vol. 1: 134–139, 1970. Clifford v. Woodford, 83 Ariz. 257, 320 P2d 452 (1957). See also: Paton v. Paton, 363 Mich. 192, 108 N.W. 2d 876 (1961): Thein v. Squires, 250 Iowa 1149, 97 N.W. 2d 156 (1959); Giacopelli v. Florence Crittenton Home, 16 Ill. 2d 556, 158 N.E. 2d 613 (1959)

CASEFINDING

The recent change in the reporting statute of the Commonwealth of Massachusetts expands the number of professionals required to report cases of abuse and neglect of children; it should more adequately include the many interfaces involving children and society.[3] The health care industry and the schools remain the two major sources that should be expected to reveal the vulnerable child, the needy, stressed parents, the chaotic family, the deprived, and the abused or the neglected child.

It is necessary to effect service links among personnel in medical care, schools, and social agencies. These "horizontal linkages" should produce a cooperative team model that offers (1) mutual support to individual caretakers, (2) improved communication about the various facts of individual family needs, and (3) earlier intervention, all based on adequate casefinding and reporting of previously unrecognized and new cases of abuse and neglect of children.

The addition of a mental health worker to the office staff of pediatric practitioners would provide an appropriate professional, trained to elicit the information necessary to recognize the needful parent and to determine the needs of an abused or neglected child. Appropriate tracers must be defined and used in order that high-risk situations can be identified and closely monitored. The adolescent mother, the premature infant, and the illegitimate infant are known to be at risk. Existing protocols for health maintenance visits are not sufficient to meet the needs of these groups. Individual protocols must be established to meet the "caring" needs of these families.

When provided with the opportunity, abusive parents will frequently find relief in acknowledging the presence of the family problem; they will be receptive to intervention. This acknowledgement constitutes an important first step which can take place because of the care provider-patient relationship.

COORDINATION OF SERVICES

The recognition of vulnerability, neglect, or abuse can occur with an improved team model of health care. In the suburbs, a pediatrician, nurse practitioner, and mental health worker collaborating and working in a single office can accomplish much more than these three disciplines working separately or from designated area-wide offices. The opportunity to recognize the unmet needs of each family and its individual members should provide the insight necessary to provide appropriate

---

3. MGLA Ch. 119-51.

programs for the target child, for the parents, and for siblings of the target child.

The opportunity to refer a difficult family—where abuse or neglect is an issue—to a hospital can achieve several goals. Hospital admission affords protection of the child. If the hospital is geographically removed from the family's own community, the anonymity of the family can be preserved. Delivery of the multiple diagnostic and treatment services required by these families can be accomplished in a coordinated team model.

RECOMMENDATIONS

In order to defuse a predicament that is "anxiety-provoking" for caretakers—and especially for physicians—the following recommendations are made:

1. Educational programs should be made available to physicians, nurses, school personnel, and social agencies to acquaint them with the current reporting laws that pertain to intervention on behalf of neglected or abused children. Information relating to the process of investigation and intervention, as well as the organizational charts of the responsible public and private agencies, should be disseminated.

2. Community-based service agencies, including social service, mental health, physical health, and school, should develop reliable channels of communications. They should, in fact, develop outreach capabilities to reach the socially isolated family and, particularly, to recognize the susceptible child. The issue of confidentiality should not represent an obstacle to recognizing the abused child and responding to the best interests of that child. In addition, close cooperation between suburban community health care agencies and urban-situated hospitals, as well as public and private social agencies, can provide the large range of services required by these families.

3. It is essential that future family care-oriented physicians, nurses, and school personnel (including teachers, guidance counselors, and administrators) be provided knowledge and experience in family development, child rearing practices, and recognition of aberrant behavior which reflects family psychopathology. The practice of pediatrics has always involved the social sciences; to an increasing extent, behavioral issues do constitute the basis for concern to families and caretakers who must respond to the needs of individual family members.

4. Any legislative act which mandates earlier interaction with children to assure normal growth and development—interventive and corrective programs prior to school age—provides additional opportunities to assess the individual family's quality of life and to provide

to parents additional education on child rearing. This lack of information has constituted a major deficit in the educational experiences of growing children, adolescents, and young adults.

5. The responsible agency to accept reports and deliver services to a family where child neglect or abuse has been recognized is frequently a state-supported public child welfare department. This agency is frequently understaffed; it may contract with private agencies to assist in managing the numbers of cases being reported. The state legislature must ensure a public policy that will meet defined needs with adequate resources, especially personnel. Consultative services such as psychiatric evaluation—as well as crises-oriented interventive services (for example, crisis day care services and foster grandparents or mothers' aide programs) must also be reliably funded.

SUMMARY

From Gil's work,[4] it has been evident that child abuse does exist in the large urban centers of our country. Relatively few cases are reported from suburban communities. The capacity to recognize child abuse and neglect depends upon the education of all adults from the many disciplines who interact with children and families in the course of their daily activities. In suburban communities, responsible intervention and responsive, innovative programs to meet these individual families' needs depend upon the communication and coordination of services among physicians, nurses, social workers, social agencies, hospitals, schools, lawyers, and courts. In addition, the state legislature must enact laws to provide the funds to maintain and expand service programs to infants, children and adolescents—as well as their parents—who are involved in the complex syndromes of abuse and neglect. The ultimate goal is to maintain the integrity of the family unit and improve the quality of interpersonal relationships among its individual members so that the cycle of inappropriate child rearing can be finally interrupted and dismantled.

---

4. Gil, D. G. *Violence Against Children.* Cambridge: Harvard University Press, 1973.

PART THREE

RECOGNIZING AND DEALING WITH EMOTIONAL REACTIONS TO CHILD ABUSE

5 Attitudes of Professionals in the Management and Treatment of Child Abuse

Joanne D. Lipner, ACSW

Janine was brought to the emergency room of a large teaching hospital in the Boston area. Her parents and the family public assistance worker accompanied the child. The account given to the admitting physician was that Janine had lost consciousness after having been left in a bathtub of icy water. Upon examination, it was discovered that Janine had sustained a broken arm, several rib fractures, multiple lacerations and bruises; she was seriously malnourished. Janine was diagnosed as a battered child. She was then four years old.

This chapter discusses my experience as a social worker in the public protective agency with Janine and her family. In this case, the dynamics that very often occur among professionals involved in the management and treatment of child abuse are particularly apparent.

My first contact with the O'Brien family was two years after Janine's hospitalization. She was then experiencing her third foster home placement; she also had been in and out of her natural parents' home. My initial visit with Mr. and Mrs. O'Brien was characterized by their frank hostility. I went to their home on several occasions before I was permitted entry—and then it was only to let me know that they would

31

not work with me. Mrs. O'Brien presented herself as overwhelmingly depressed and Mr. O'Brien as an impulsive, overtly angry man. As Janine was in placement and her immediate safety was not an issue, I let the O'Briens know that I would return to their home upon request. I also made it clear that I would set aside a definite time every week that would be theirs to use or not to use. I would be available from ten to eleven every Tuesday morning; I could be reached then at my office should they reconsider.

Before long, I began to receive telephone calls from Mrs. O'Brien during this time. At first it was only to test out whether in fact I was available during that hour; then she called to talk with me for increasing periods of time. Finally, Mrs. O'Brien requested a home visit. In a rather classic way, this sequence illustrates the O'Briens' need to feel in control of a situation. Given that control, they felt free to move towards help. Then ensued a series of weekly visits with me, designed to evaluate their readiness to plan for Janine's future.

As I came to know the O'Briens, I came to appreciate their mistrust of helping professionals. It became apparent early in my relationship with this couple that their beginning contacts with both physicians and social service agencies had been negative. Mr. and Mrs. O'Brien had been requesting placement of Janine for more than two years before her hospitalization. It is both interesting and tragic that the local community agencies from which they sought assistance were unresponsive to their desperate request. Both parents were explicit in their verbalized fear of killing their own child. I wonder how ready we are as professionals to recognize the reality of child abuse when we cannot hear and respond to a direct cry for help—much less become alert to and recognize unverbalized messages.

Upon arrival at the hospital, Janine was quickly separated from her parents. Mr. and Mrs. O'Brien were not permitted to see her; they were told by the admitting physician that, if he had anything to do with it, they would never see Janine again. This couple reacted to their experience at the hospital by closing themselves off to professional help —alienating themselves even further from what they perceived as a hostile and threatening world.

Of course, it is quite natural to be shocked and angry when child abuse occurs; certainly, protection of the child is essential. However, unrecognized feelings of anger in professionals can deter any therapeutic efforts with the parents. No matter how the parents present themselves, their expectations are that they will be cast in the role of "bad" parents. To this underlying fear and hurt we must address ourselves.

The O'Brien family was referred to the Department of Public Welfare under the child abuse reporting statute by the hospital social worker. There was enormous pressure on the social worker by medical staff to effect a safe and speedy solution to Janine's life situation. In addition, the social worker found the O'Briens demanding, hostile, and frustrating. Her unrecognized anxiety in dealing with this couple was transferred to the public agency social worker who, in turn, reacted by communicating inappropriately with Mr. and Mrs. O'Brien, meeting their hostility with hostility.

The vicious cycle thus set in motion resulted in a battle of wills between the O'Briens and the public protective agency, during which time Janine suffered most of all. In reaction to rigid limit setting and what was perceived as rejection by the authority agency, the O'Briens responded by sabotaging Janine's foster home placement and demanding her return to their home. Receiving Janine home—and, of course, not having worked out the root of their problem with Janine—they would re-experience feelings of rage towards her and demand another placement.

It took weeks that stretched into months for Mr. and Mrs. O'Brien to let down their wall of hostility and begin a relationship that had some element of trust. Continued weekly sessions which focused on issues and feelings in the O'Briens' past and present relationship with Janine led to frequent visits and, ultimately, to the return of Janine to their care. Both parents were firm in their conviction that, being cognizant of the underlying reasons for their abuse of Janine, they could cope with their feelings—positive and negative—toward her. They had been asking me for help in other family crises, and they felt certain that they could anticipate difficulty with Janine and use help when needed.

Upon Janine's return to her parents, the door shut again. Some three weeks later, Mr. and Mrs. O'Brien let me know that they did not feel our visits were helpful; they would be terminating their involvement with me. Janine was already regressing in her behaviour, and I knew the O'Briens would not use other community supports. Again, I let them know that I would be available to them and, also, that I would not accept their decision at this time. Nevertheless, I could not force them to use help. Perhaps they needed to try things on their own for a while.

This rejection of the help offered is reflective of where the O'Briens were in their own process. Once the beginning of a trusting relationship has been established, it is expected that abusive parents will run again. We must be able to recognize that these families have always found that those to whom they have turned for help usually disappoint and hurt them. Soon I was receiving telephone calls at the agency and at home. Again, the O'Briens had to test out the reality of my availability to them and to renew their trust in my commitment to work with them. Once more I began weekly home visits.

It was at this point that the importance of professional collaboration became crucial. I was involved as the protective worker. Others involved were the public assistance worker, the school adjustment counselor, the school nurse, Janine's teacher, and medical and social service staff from the hospital where the O'Brien family was referred. Before long, I learned that Janine was being examined for possible bruises on a daily basis by the school nurse. The public assistance worker was making visits without appointment to the family, and the school adjustment counselor was telephoning my office with repeated inquiries as to Janine's safety at home.

It was not too long before I began to feel uneasy with the situation and somewhat unsure of my role as caseworker for the O'Brien family. As my doubts increased, so did my anxiety. I re-examined my work with this family and affirmed my decision to return Janine to her parents; I felt strongly that she was safe with them. It soon became apparent to me that an *unusual* but fairly *typical* dynamic pattern had developed among the professionals involved with this family. My uneasiness stemmed primarily from the high-level anxiety a child abuse case arouses in those who work closely with the family. My recognition of my feelings as related to Janine's being with her parents enabled me to become aware that this anxiety was indeed operative in others. It was certainly manifested by professionals examining Janine daily at the school, dropping in on the family unannounced, and, in general, projecting all responsibility for Janine's safety onto me.

There was also a subtle but clear implication from the other professionals that, as a protective worker in a public agency, I could not be considered to be a social work professional. This absence of support from the community agencies reflected for me what the O'Briens must have experienced so much more intensely. My frustration was only heightened as I continued to work with this couple in their struggle to relate more appropriately to Janine. I began to "run interference" for the family with the hospital, the school, and the welfare department—feeling that I had to "protect" them from any further punitive treatment.

As Kempe and Helfer note in their book, *Helping the Battered Child and His Family,* "The presence or lack of communication among all concerned can make or break a case." [1] There was certainly concern among all the professionals involved. Communication and support for one another were missing—not to mention an understanding of the dynamics present in this particular family system. Again, hostility on the O'Briens part was met with hostility—or worse yet, with patronizing sympathy.

My later attempts to establish communication were somewhat successful. I was able to clarify my own role and, through consistent contact

---

1. Kempe, C. H. and Helfer, R. E., eds. *Helping the Battered Child and His Family.* Philadelphia: Lippincott, 1972.

with the community agencies, develop professional trust in Janine's placement at home. As the tension diminished among the principal helping persons, we were better able to collaborate with one another and to coordinate more effective service to the family. Nevertheless, shared responsibility for the case did not bring about attitudinal changes towards the family. I stopped "running interference" in both the professional and lay communities and focused my attention on enabling the O'Briens to deal with the rejection and hostility they still experience—to this day.

Janine has been in her own home for three years. The protective agency has closed its case, and Mr. and Mrs. O'Brien and Janine are in out-patient therapy at the same hospital where Janine was diagnosed a battered child.

One of the basic learning experiences gained in working with this family was that appropriate professional attitudes toward families where child abuse occurs is a long way off. A long-term goal with Mr. and Mrs. O'Brien was to encourage them to risk giving professionals a chance. Mr. and Mrs. O'Brien achieved a hard-won sense of self-worth as individuals and as parents. At times, this achievement occurred in spite of their experiences with helping professionals. We need to listen carefully to what abusive parents perceive as help; we must look carefully and become aware of our own feelings toward child abuse. Awareness is a prelude to becoming responsible for these feelings and to starting to use ourselves differently in our work with abused children and their parents.

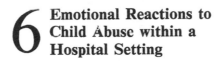

6 Emotional Reactions to Child Abuse within a Hospital Setting

Deborah A. Hill, MSW

When an abused child is admitted to a hospital, a whole variety of emotional reactions are set in motion. The manner in which these feelings are understood and handled has great impact on the treatment process and outcome.

On the part of the admitting physicians and nurses, a natural response of horror arises from the injuries they see—outrage that these have been inflicted on a helpless victim and, additionally, anger at the alleged perpetrators of these injuries. It may be immediately evident that the child is permanently damaged. If so, this fact increases the physician's feelings of helplessness; it hinders his desire to return his patient to good health and thus enhances his feelings of anger and frustration.

All of these feelings make it extremely difficult for the medical staff to deal directly and compassionately with the parent at this time; the parent is more likely treated with silence or thinly concealed tension as he is directed from the emergency ward to the inpatient floor. This shroud of silence and avoidance may continue for a very long time while attention focuses on treatment of the child's injuries and while the medical staff struggles with how to face the parent. The parent is then dealt with in a variety of ways, ranging from direct angry accusations or thinly veiled but polite questioning, to more positive direct confrontation accompanied by verbal concern for the parent and his or her situation. The medical staff's natural desire to protect the child from this outrageous treatment may result in a strong conviction on the physician's part that the only solution to this problem is placement—that to be party to the child's return home is only to expose him to continued maltreatment.

Hospital admission of a battered child thus takes on strong feelings of urgency and crisis; these feelings on the part of staff members are communicated in a demand that something be done to alleviate the situation. Frequently, a magical expectation is placed on the social worker. The staff wants this professional somehow to produce a simple, immediate happy ending out of a complex abusive situation created possibly by years of misery. The wish arises from the extreme frustration and helplessness experienced by those dealing with the problem. An actual or imagined threat of a parent removing a child from the hospital against medical advice causes the feelings of urgency to increase.

Generally during admission of an abused child, an immediate referral has been made to hospital social service. The social worker receives an urgent call for help—a deluge of the medical staff's feelings, of their concerns, and of their urgent desires to protect the child and effect a satisfactory outcome. The social worker experiences a good deal of pressure from this first contact; he or she must, of course, deal with a personal feelings of outrage and a wish to protect an innocent victim.

The pressure on the social worker to act swiftly may be increased by a medical situation which requires only a brief hospital stay. Artificially prolonged hospitalization can combine with bed shortages to deprive other medically needy patients of care. Sometimes a long hospital stay creates an unhealthy situation for child and family; it is, of course, a very expensive way to effect a needed separation while careful evaluation and plans are carried out. However, the dearth of emergency care facilities for children makes this choice a serious dilemma.

The hospital social worker sees the family to begin an evaluation of problems so extensive that they have resulted in a serious symptom—child abuse. She must assess the family's strengths and weaknesses and its capacity to accept help toward providing future care and protection for this child. In this same interview, she must begin to develop a positive caring relationship with parents who feel frightened, guilty, overwhelmed with personal problems, and convinced that no one could possibly be interested in helping them. Very frequently the parents' defensive structure takes the form of denial and hostility, making the positive relationship goal a difficult one. Anxiety generated by the need for decision making in protective cases is high. Often the social worker must make a differential diagnosis when medical data do not rule out accidental injury. In this case, interviewing skills and accurate assessment of family dynamics are crucial. The social worker must decide whether the child is in a risky position and needs the help of a protective agency. Frequently, he or she must do this from relatively limited verbal data from a denying and defensive parent. The social worker must decide from the concrete data, from professional judgment arising from knowledge of human dynamics, and from his or her own emotional response to the parent.

As with any case, a number of alternatives are available, and the worker must choose a treatment plan most suited to the family's needs. This decision is very likely to be an unpopular one with someone; the results of the worker's actions may affect individual lives in a major way. Such decisions should be shared ones. They should involve consultation from supervisory or trauma team staff.

The anxiety experienced in making the above decisions does not end when the plan is made. Next, the decision must be communicated to a parent who consciously feels misunderstood, threatened, and criticized —even though at some unconscious level, he or she experiences relief from the protective action. If indicated, the worker must in this contact pave the way for a positive referral to the local child welfare agency to which the hospital must refer all cases of suspected child abuse. The worker must also help the physician endorse this referral in a positive, non-punitive discussion with the parent.

As hospitalization wears on, the patient improves or worsens, and the family makes demands on the medical staff for discharge; when no decision regarding planning has yet been made by the child welfare agency, tensions rise and increased demands are placed on the hospital social worker. He or she frequently experiences considerable conflict in trying to deal with the anxieties and pressures of the staff and the parents. He or she tries to interpret the position of the public welfare agency— which, in its overburdened condition, may be slow to respond to the needs of the family and hospital.

Additional problems arise in trying to interpret the thinking and decision-making of the welfare worker when communication is not frequent and clear or when opinions may differ and a case conference has not yet been held to share thinking. In these instances, the hospital social worker is constantly in the position of playing go-between, of being the recipient of unrealistic demands, and of telling people things they do not want to hear. The parent does not want to hear that the hospital thinks the child has been abused and, consequently, he or she is being referred to the Public Welfare Department. The Public Welfare Department does not want to hear that the hospital must press for an early discharge. The physician does not want to hear that the welfare worker does not view placement as the only alternative. However, the hospital social worker must deal with all of these increased demands while continuing to meet a normally busy schedule.

Another attitude common to hospital staff is that of apathy and helplessness. How frequently has a physician said, "Why refer this child and family to this agency when I never see any evidence of positive outcome? This will only be perceived by the family as a punitive step. They will not then return to the hospital for care, and they will receive no help." It is common for staff to forget about past positive outcomes when confronted with the crisis of a new, seemingly overwhelming case. However, this apathetic attitude has been enhanced in part by problems in communication between the Welfare Department and the referring hospital concerning: (1) the thinking that went into the agency's decision, (2) the services the agency plans to offer, and (3) later, the changes forthcoming in the family as a result of the agency's intervention. As far as the physician is concerned, that family has disappeared and that child is still in jeopardy; the physician cannot see how effective a role he or she has played.

Additional, realistic cause for apathy and discouragement is the continued lack of sufficient services available to the abusing family. While an unwitting legislature broadens the protective service regulations so that more people must refer more cases, the legislators sometimes fail to appropriate sufficient funds so that the intent of the law—to provide services such as day care and casework—can be carried out effectively. This fact frustrates everyone. However, to fail to act protectively because of this frustration is not only negligent, but it makes unavailable the data to substantiate the need by demonstrating the numbers of families requiring help.

7 Strains and Stresses in Protective Services

Paul D'Agostino, MSW

It is generally recognized by those in the helping professions that child welfare is a physically and emotionally difficult area of work. It is pregnant with professional and lay prejudices, community misunderstandings and biases, political footballs, scarcity of manpower, and inadequate resources. There is often role confusion within individual workers and among the various disciplines involved. Child welfare causes anxieties and conflicts because it challenges the worker's command of intra-personal feelings and his or her skill in inter-personal relationships.

Within the child welfare field, these problems are intensified for those involved in the protective services, especially for those dealing with the problem of child abuse. In few other areas of work are the pressure to respond immediately so intense and the consequences of that response so threatening. The purpose of this chapter is to identify and discuss some of these particular strains and stresses. Doing so does not remove them from our growing list of problems, but recognizing them is one of the first steps in being able to cope with them.

In an effort to put some order into an unorderly and diffused subject matter, we have attempted to divide these "strains and stresses" into two categories—those which are primarily intra-personal and those which are primarily inter-personal. This pragmatic categorizing will result in some overlapping in discussion.

Intra-personal strains and stresses are those difficulties which a worker experiences because of his or her personal feelings, prejudices, anxieties, and fears. These will be discussed in the next chapter. I will discuss what we have referred to as the inter-personal difficulties one experiences in this field. They stem primarily from relationships with the families one sees and the community agencies with which one works. These relationships are never totally separate from the worker's personal feelings.

First, it would help to briefly capsulize the classical description of child abuse. It is not a disease or disturbance in itself; it is a symptom and result of other problems within the family's intra- and inter-personal relationships. Consequently, the identified patient, the child, is not the main problem. The problem lies with the parent and his or her limited capacity to cope with, provide for, and relate to the child. Contrary to the popularly held belief, the ability to socially parent a child is not totally instinctual. It is a developed and learned behavior.

Frequently, parents who batter their children grew up in homes where there was a breakdown or absence of parenting and where they themselves were battered. These homes had constant tensions, frequent disruptions, and pathological relationships. As a result, many abusive parents now have unfulfilled childhood and dependency needs, preventing them from meeting their child's needs. They perceive their child as being a little adult and expect him to give to them. When the child fails to do so, they perceive this as rejection.

Abusive parents are generally insecure, anxious, and threatened in their roles as parents. They become overwhelmed by the demands their child makes of them. They often unconsciously project their own hostilities onto the one particular child who serves as the scapegoat for the family problems. Finally, they are limited in their capacity to establish any meaningful relationships, but are still involved in pathological relationships with their own parents or with other significant persons from their childhood. They are usually impulse-ridden, isolated individuals, unable to trust, with few, if any, social contacts. Taking this into account, the task of establishing a relationship with such parents appears difficult. Add to this the fact that involvement of protective services, triggered by abusive behavior to their child, is very threatening and frequently represents failure.

This task of establishing a relationship with many abusive parents is difficult, but experience has shown that it can be done. The quality of the initial contact with the family is crucial and will set the tone of the relationship. Experience has proved that abusive parents must be treated with respect, dignity, and an understanding of their problems. To do this calls for constructive and supportive inter-agency communication and team work. A child welfare worker has often suffered otherwise preventable difficulty because of the quality of the family's initial contacts with other helping agencies. In a non-threatening, non-condemning and supportive manner, we must tell the family why we are involved. This initial honesty about the reason for the referral is helpful to the family and can later save difficulty and confusion about our role during the course of treatment. Families should be allowed the right to verbally deny their abusive behavior to the child. They should be encouraged to focus instead on their problems and immediate concerns. Other problems in establishing and maintaining a relationship arise out of the parents' anxieties, and often guilt, denial, projection, and inability to engage in meaningful, trusting relationships.

Other difficulties may come about as a result of extended family involvement. Frequently, when gains are made and the family begins to show improvement and independence in functioning, problems arise with the extended family members who become threatened and attempt to sabotage the relationship and the gains which the family has made. We must be alert to this possibility as it can put clients in an emotional bind, forcing them to choose between their worker and their family before they are emotionally equipped to handle such a problem. The worker's awareness and anticipation of this aids in his or her ability to remain out of such a triangle and to be supportive of the client through this period. To do so, we cannot have confidences with other family members. What grandmother may say cannot be held in confidence from mother when mother is the client. Such a situation may present many problems and must be clarified and handled immediately. Little secrets with family members quickly become major problems and undermine basic trust and honesty. By the same token, clients must know and believe that what they discuss with us is held in confidence and is not mentioned to extended family members without their knowledge and approval. Again basic honesty is an essential component of our work with the family and must be present and ongoing from the time of initial involvement.

The majority of the strains and stresses one experiences do not just arrive out of the worker-client relationship. Neither the worker, nor the family being seen, live or work in a vacuum. Families may frequently be involved in problems of housing, education, nutrition, financing, drugs, alcohol, health, or retardation. Their friends or companions may be destructive influences and their way of life chaotic. These problems put pressure on the client and the worker, and a feeling of being overwhelmed can quickly become contagious. "If only this didn't happen" or "If only that weren't there" become frequently used expressions. The danger of becoming caught up in the client's chaos is ever present. We may begin to feel frustrated, angry, and sometimes at "wits' end."

One of the first things we must do is sort out responsibilities. What can we do to help this family? What changes can we help bring about and what things are outside our capacity to alter? Always remember, that what we have no control over, we cannot accept responsibility for, even though others might try to impose this responsibility on us. This seems very simple, but a feeling of total responsibility can become one of the most difficult problems. It will cause extreme pressure which will lead only to frustration.

The question of responsibility is always a difficult one. The case responsibility consists of providing protection for the child and help for the family. The exact nature and extent of this varies with each individual case but it cannot be the sole responsibility of any one person or even of any one agency. This responsibility must be a shared one; some of the greatest periods of stress can come from the lack of such sharing. This brings us directly to those problems which can arise from working relationships with other agencies and disciplines. The fact that we must work with other agencies can, at times, be a great help and comfort or, at other times, can be a headache. Difficulties arise in two main areas: the inability or unwillingness of an agency to respond, and disagreement over what action should be taken.

Very realistically, there is a general manpower shortage in most agencies. Demand is greater than the ability to respond. Added to this is the limited number of resources available. These two factors present an ongoing frustration to the protective service worker. Their remedy lies in group and legislative action and requires a reassessment of our national and state priorities. Until such time, they will continue to be a difficult and ever-present problem. Other agencies tend to be fearful of an involvement in a child abuse situation. They need education and support in accepting this community responsibility for working with such families.

The second area of difficulty or disagreement over what action should be taken is far more complicated. It involves individual personalities, needs, and trust. Each discipline and agency involved with a case must respect the expertise of the others involved and must work toward the betterment of the referred family. Mutual trust and respect are essential. If a recognized team or group of agencies is attempting to make a decision on a case, that team must jointly share the responsibility for the decision and its implementation. One of the most potentially difficult and frustrating experiences is to have a group make a decision for whose implementation one worker is totally responsible. This stands out most sharply with decisions made around placement and court involvement.

The question of placement and court is a difficult and emotional one. Mutual respect is crucial, and there must be a sharing of responsibility for this decision and its implementation. The team cannot be used to dictate what should be done and then shift that responsibility to one person. This is not responsibility sharing, yet it is frequently a situation in which the protective service worker finds himself or herself. The worker is then thrown into a conflicting role with the family and is caught in a difficult and stressful bind.

Again, disagreement on decision-making and lack of responsibility sharing are two of the greatest problems in inter-agency relations. What is needed is an inter-agency, inter-disciplinary team which not only shares decision-making but also shares the responsibility for ongoing implementation of decisions. This team must have known and accepted criteria for the decisions being made and mutual respect for individual team members and the disciplines which they represent.

We have briefly discussed many of the strains and stresses which are experienced in the field of protective service. Some we can avoid, some we can lessen, and others we just have to ride out. We should not take them personally and we should not take them home. We must take support from each other and comfort in knowing that we are not alone.

8 Preventing Strains and Stresses in Protective Services

Nancy B. Ebeling, ACSW

Child abuse and child neglect are emotionally charged subjects. Think for a moment about your own reactions when a child's hand is held over a lighted burner to teach him not to play with matches. Consider the child who at three years weighs 16 pounds due to lack of food and care. What about the baby who is thrown against a wall, or hit, and whose body is a mass of bruises and broken bones. What about the baby and his two-year-old sister who have been left alone night after night with a babysitter who is their six-year-old brother. It isn't easy for anyone to look at such situations without some reaction. The important issue is how we deal with our attitudes and feelings in order to understand and help parents who probably were subjected to similar kind of mistreatment when they were children.

Child abuse and neglect does indeed produce a variety of reactions and attitudes; it can easily result in subjective thinking. We know that attitudes toward any problem create the climate. If our attitudes are subjective, punishing, angry, or confused, the climate will be negative and more destructive than helping. If, however, our attitudes are objective, understanding, and helpful, then we create an atmosphere in which we can be of real service to the children and families with whom we come in contact.

I would like to discuss some of the feelings and attitudes we all have in working with families who are neglectful or abusive of their children and how we can cope with some of these inner stresses in order to feel more comfortable and to be more helpful. I think it's important to review, however, some very basic ingredients that are essential in working with any person coming for service. Awareness of these areas is necessary to deal successfully with the complex problems of abuse and neglect.

We are unable to approach a problem in a coordinated and helpful way if our own biases and personal conflicts stand in the way. Self-awareness, therefore, is basic to our really knowing and understanding others. We cannot fully understand others until we understand our own attitudes; we cannot be comfortable in helping others with their fears and anxieties unless we are comfortable with ourselves.

There is a human tendency to project pleasant and unpleasant emotions onto others. The degree to which this projection takes place with our clients or patients is of vital importance. Clearly, we cannot superimpose our values on others or expect of them what we expect of ourselves. To project our emotional needs onto others will actually defeat our real purpose, which should be helping an individual realize his own potential. It is our responsibility to study and be aware of our own reactions in order to maintain objectivity and to be as emotionally free as possible in our relationships with those to whom we are giving service. The kind of relationship to which we refer here is the getting together of two persons for the purpose of assisting one of them—the patient or client—toward adjustment of a personal problem.

In this kind of relationship, which encompasses all that happens between the participants (feelings, thoughts, actions, etc.) there are really two levels of emotional exchange. One is reality, which relates to the current situation; it is felt by both parties and is a reaction to something which happens in the present. For example, Mrs. B becomes angry because the interview is interrupted by some phone calls to the worker. She is realistically annoyed, and she says so.

The other familiar level of exchange is the transference process in which the client or patient places on the worker feelings which relate to someone or to some experiences in the client's past life. The transference can be in the form of a negative or positive reaction; it may just as likely occur in a short-term relationship as in a deeper treatment relationship.

Consider a rather simple example: Mrs. J has a good relationship with the worker and, after several home visits, wants the worker to "help" a friend of hers in the next apartment. Seeing this request as positive, the worker agrees to do so; she sees Mrs. J's friend twice, referring her to a clinic. The contacts take place each time after leaving Mrs. J's apartment. For no apparent reason, Mrs. J breaks one appointment and became rather quiet in subsequent interviews. Closer examination of Mrs. J's family situation shows that she had a foster sister with whom her mother used to have long talks and whom she thought her mother favored. It appears that the worker's two visits to her neighbor and friend led to the change in Mrs. J's attitude and to the broken appointment. Her reaction to the situation was similar to the way in which she dealt with a past experience in her life in which she had to share her mother with an unrelated person. The understanding by the worker and her subsequent discussion with Mrs. J succeeded in keeping the original relationship intact. Transference is a normal and natural phenomenon; it must be taken into account in any relationship.

The other side of the coin is the counter-transference—the feelings of the worker as they come out of past experiences and relationships and are projected onto the client. Although this is not a natural or healthy phenomenon and it can be harmful to the relationship, it is not uncommon. In counter-transference, the worker acts out of his own needs to the detriment of the client. He may, for example, forget appointments, be critical, deny money, be reluctant to raise certain issues, become anxious, or be too giving or too protective. Clearly, any person involved in a helping relationship must understand counter-transference so as to develop objectivity in work with clients or patients and, through understanding, prevent or minimize the possibility of its occurring.

Sensitivity to emotional reactions and an understanding of transference and counter-transference will help us to avoid many of the various stresses and strains in protective services.

Many other factors in the areas of neglect and abuse, however, can influence our attitudes and emotional reactions more strongly than other relationships and can test us to the maximum. As we mentioned earlier, we can become upset and angry that a child has been hurt by an adult. One reaction may be to "rescue" the child and overlook his parents' problems. With this kind of approach, of course, the child will undoubtedly be the loser in the long run. Or, in another kind of reaction, the problem of neglect or abuse is denied or minimized by the observer—perhaps because he cannot bear to recognize the problem for what it is because if he does, he will then have to do something about it, either by dealing with the family in a direct way or by making a referral to an appropriate agency.

Becoming involved with families who are not adequately protecting their children, or who have actually abused a child, can and does arouse a lot of anxiety. We may have mixed feelings about possibly infringing on parents' rights, or their privacy, or perhaps our own feelings about authority may get in the way. Also present may be a feeling of insecurity regarding our skill in handling situations which may arouse overt hostility or aggressiveness toward us by another person.

There are those professionals working in agencies whose function —or one of whose functions—it is to provide protective services. Others work in settings which, while they do not offer protective services per se, do come in contact with children who are at risk. Such children may well be part of families being seen by a variety of agencies or institutions such as mental health centers, family and children agencies, courts, schools, medical facilities, physicians, etc. Many who work in these settings will discover that some form of neglect or abuse exists within some or many of the families seen. Then a responsibility arises either to work with the family in a manner which will help them resolve the problems to an acceptable degree or to refer the family to an agency which can and will offer help and protection to the family.

It is generally not appropriate, however, for an agency or institution which is already working closely with a family to refer it elsewhere because of neglect or abuse. These are symptoms of family dysfunctioning; they should be treated as part of the whole. Each family should be viewed on an individual basis, and the planning done accordingly to the needs of that family. Again, it is important that each of us professionally involved with a family carefully examines his or her attitudes about parents who mistreat their children; we must realize how these attitudes can seriously influence our approach to the problem and to the decisions we make on behalf of a family.

One of the real difficulties which occurs is the uneasiness we sometimes feel about talking directly to a family about the problem. We may really feel the weight of this responsibility, but we can only be helpful when the problem is approached in an honest, non-judgmental, clearly defined manner. Sometimes a reluctance to deal with child abuse arises because we are fearful that it will interrupt an already ongoing relationship in a setting where a person has voluntarily come for service. Actually though, if talking over such problems with a family interferes with the relationship, then perhaps the relationship was already tenuous or in jeopardy. Much of the time, however, this fear is a projection of one's own anxieties onto the family; in most instances, if handled properly, the parents are relieved to have the problems discussed and to get help, even though they may at first deny the problem or appear angry and resistant. Many situations, however, are complex; we can feel frustrated and anxious about working out a plan for a family. It can be a stressful situation for the person dealing with the problem, as well as for the family—but it will be made easier for both if the worker has an open mind which is free of biases and other emotional barriers.

When a family is referred to an agency dealing mainly with child abuse and neglect, that agency—although it must definitely have community back-up to be effective—pretty much takes on the responsibility of protecting the child or children in the family. This big responsibility is felt keenly by the worker giving service to the family. Various community pressures often operate as large external forces. The internal pressures of feeling responsible is also quite often very anxiety-provoking. No individual should be placed in this position alone. He or she must feel the agency's support—through a supervisor mainly, but also through the total agency structure. It is unfair to both family and worker for one person to carry a burden not shared with another responsible person.

Although the parents with whom we work have varying degrees of ego strengths, many are severely deprived emotionally; out of their dependency needs, they place great demands on a worker's patience, tolerance, and disposition. Each person should know his or her own tolerance level and have some sort of a safety valve available. When we feel exhausted emotionally and physically at the end of a day after home visits (through rain, snow, or mud) that may have involved several crises, screaming children, arguing parents, sticky fingers, a hostile mother, and disgruntled neighbors, it is not easy to sit down and think about transference and counter-transference or to take stock of our emotions and reactions to the events of the day. If we can develop self-discipline to do this, however, it does pay dividends in the long run. Stopping a minute now and then to think, look, and listen can be helpful in regaining equilibrium and in reducing anxiety and frustration so that the next time around some of the strains and stresses lessen. This analysis may be easier said than done, but actually, if it is done, things are really easier! Time spent in this way enables us to be more effective with our families, and it does reduce the amount of emotional drain that can occur.

In summary, then—self-awareness and insight into our feelings will help us to be more effective. If we are handicapped by our own emotional hang-ups, we only add to the existing stresses and strains and make them more complicated. Attitudes which are positive, and which do not include value judgments and vested interests, will free us to offer a realistic and sensitive approach to families.

PART FOUR

PROGRAM MANAGEMENT IN THE MEDICAL SETTING

9 The Collaborative Aspect of the Hospital Social Worker's Role

Anne E. McDonald, ACSW

During the hospitalization of an abused child, the hospital social worker becomes directly involved with the child, the parents, and sometimes other family members. This interaction serves a diagnostic purpose, and it often contributes significantly to the evolution of a viable treatment plan. There is, however, another aspect to the hospital social worker's role during this period. This further dimension is the collaboration with other persons concerned in treating the family, both within the hospital and without.

Before describing the specifics of this collaboration, I think it might be helpful to add some comments on the child-abusing population. The majority of reported child abuse cases are diagnosed in the emergency rooms of large, inner-city hospitals. The chief advantage which the urban hospital enjoys in diagnosing child abuse is the fairly impersonal relationship it shares with its consumers. In most instances, the staff of an urban hospital is not well acquainted with the families being served; it thus can be reasonably objective when identifying a case of child abuse. (This situation is pointed out to us occasionally when we are forced to acknowledge that a family well known to us—at least on a superficial

55

basis—is involved in a battering situation. In such cases, we frequently suffer from nagging feelings that we have betrayed this family and that we are being punitive when reporting it to the appropriate social agency.)

Another facet of the urban hospital experience is that the majority of the families using our clinics and emergency rooms are neither affluent nor sophisticated. Clearly, there may well be enormous external differences in the clientele referred by a private physician to a rural or suburban hospital and the clientele usually seen in an urban emergency room. Knowing your patients on a first-name basis, being confronted by the protective veneer afforded by affluence and/or sophistication—such are added obstacles in the already difficult path toward identification and treatment of child abuse cases.

The important fact to remember, however, is that basically the human equation is the same. The components of a stressful situation —isolation from significant others, turning to a child to meet dependency needs a child can never meet—are constant in battering parents, no matter what their socio-economic status may be. Therefore, the majority of suggestions being made can readily be translated for use in any hospital setting by any hospital social worker.

This discussion of collaboration may well begin with an outline of the family evaluation process used by many hospitals in dealing with cases of child abuse. The generally preferred method of in-depth assessment includes hospitalization of the injured child, whether medically necessary or not. While the child is being treated, the parents and other members of the family unit are assessed by observation, and skilled interviews are conducted by the hospital's interdisciplinary trauma team. The data received are then used in developing an ongoing treatment plan for the whole family. In formulating this plan, the team is often assisted by community agencies who have known the family in the past and who are willing to take part in the proposed therapy.

During the period of evaluation, the hospital social worker must deal with several problems resulting from hospitalization of the child and bearing directly on the eventual success or failure of family treatment. Overcoming parental resistance to intervention is usually the paramount problem; next in difficulty is the problem of coping with staff attitudes toward the battered child and his parents. "Staff" can be anyone from housekeeping personnel to a visiting medical specialist—any person employed by the hospital with whom the battering family comes in contact.

Predictably, staff members who have neither an appreciation of the dynamics of child abuse nor an opportunity to get to know the battering parents will develop a distorted picture of the phenomenon. Their distortion will have three elements: (1) the child being best served by permanent removal from his or her former environment; (2) the parents as totally depraved individuals with no redeeming human qualities; and (3) consciously or unconsciously, the staff member as the child's would-be rescuer and savior.

My experience has been that by and large the hospital staff is most pleased when a battered child is removed from his family. When a severely abused child is returned to his parents disapproval will be voiced long and loud—usually by staff members not directly working with the family and usually toward the hospital social worker as the person somehow most culpable. This disapproval is not easy to live with.

Obviously, the hospital social worker can't get involved in an apologia for every unpopular decision made by the trauma team. It would be a gross violation of a family's right to confidentiality, as well as an activity which could occupy every working hour. A better approach would be to inaugurate a series of talks for various groups within the hospital on the causes of battering, the ways in which such families can be helped, and the dangers inherent in separating a child from his family. In a teaching facility, it is usually easy enough to secure an invitation to speak to groups of medical or nursing students. Also, the trauma team should regularly describe its function to incoming house officers and new members of the nursing service.

While busily improving the attitude of other staff members, the hospital social worker must remember to keep a weather eye on his or her own feelings. Battering parents present themselves in a variety of manners, but the overall initial impression is not generally favorable. They tend to be self-centered, immature, seemingly unconcerned about their child's health, and worried most about what will happen to them. They are also likely to be hostile, defensive, and verbally abusive. They may threaten the worker—with legal reprisals, if they are somewhat sophisticated, or with physical injury if they are operating on a more simple level. Either way, a climate of violence and loss of control may frighten and repel the hospital social worker.

The need for frequent reflection on personal emotions and reactions toward battering parents is obvious. If actions or demeanor convey rejection to these parents, it will naturally have an adverse effect on their availability to treatment. Moreover, the professional's distaste for these parents can communicate itself to other staff members, who may well adopt the same attitude.

Probably the most valuable contribution a hospital can make to beginning therapy with a battering family is to demonstrate a concern for the parents as individuals and an interest in their problem, as well as those of the child. The onus is upon the hospital social worker to take the lead in making such parents feel accepted—seeing that they are aware of visiting hours and making them feel welcome on the wards, even if they must be accompanied when they visit. They must be kept abreast of the child's medical progress, just like the parents of a patient with a more traditional illness. Rather than zeroing in on the needs of the child per se, the approach should stress participation in the child's hospital care as a factor contributing to the child's recovery and as their right as parents. In this way, the hospitalization becomes a tool in rebuilding the parents' damaged self-esteem.

Frequently, numerous individuals from community agencies who have prior knowledge of the family can assist the hospital in selecting the appropriate manner of intervention. Battering families often engage in the practice of hospital and social agency "shopping"—going from one to the next as crises present themselves. The hospital social worker should recognize this tendency, try to find out where the family has been before, and assess the results of these contacts with other agencies and health care facilities. As well as affording valuable background information about a family, such inquiries can often prevent duplication of services. For example, if the family is known to a neighborhood health clinic—and the clinic is willing to take on the responsibility of carefully monitoring the entire family's health care—it would be foolish for the hospital to set up its own elaborate arrangement of pediatric follow-up for the battered child alone.

Agency representatives who have known the family in the past often see the family in a completely different context from that of the hospital; they can add new perspectives to the trauma team's evaluation. How a family has coped with past stresses, its members' strengths and weaknesses as seen in the community, whether or not they have been able to utilize help which has been offered—all these factors can weigh heavily in determining the components of a treatment plan. Therefore, it behooves the hospital social worker to make sure that these agency representatives are invited to participate in the dispositional conference held by the trauma team.

Child abuse is symptomatic of a complex family sickness with no simple cure. An effective course of treatment demands the pooled resources of specialists in several disciplines. The hospital's trauma team is a group of such specialists who meet regularly to deal with all the cases of child abuse which come to the hospital's attention. Pediatrician, nurse, psychiatrist, social worker, psychologist, lawyer, and administrator —each views the problems of the particular family being assessed from the vantage point of his or her own discipline. Representatives from the local child welfare agencies which bear the legal responsibility for evaluating each reported case of child abuse also participate as team members. This basic group is joined, from time to time, by representatives from other agencies who know the family being considered. All contribute to the fund of knowledge about a family from which a treatment plan eventually emerges.

In addition to the professionals involved, it is most helpful for a hospital trauma team to employ a data coordinator. The coordinator takes over many of the essential but time-consuming organizational tasks which are necessary if a trauma team is to be effective—for example, (1) completing history sheets on each family, (2) scheduling dispositional conferences, and (3) arranging periodic reviews of each case.

In a group fortunate enough to have the services of such a person, the hospital social worker's role in the trauma team is the traditional one of providing a social assessment of the family unit. Without a data coordinator, all team members can share these chores; they do not automatically become the hospital social worker's obligation.

Besides participating in the trauma team's evaluation, the hospital social worker also collaborates directly with staff from other facilities to ease the transition of the battering family from the hospital setting into long-term therapy—for example, introducing the protective service's worker to the parents or taking the family to visit a prospective day care center.

In conclusion, hospitalization of the battered child presents the hospital social worker with an excellent opportunity for time-limited crisis intervention. During this period, collaborative efforts with other concerned persons may be as important as direct interaction with the family in working toward the goal of improved family functioning. Once a period of acute hospitalization is over, this role will probably be a very secondary one in the long-range treatment of the family. However, if the hospital social worker has managed to demonstrate a spirit of caring for the battering parents as individuals and thus made it possible for them to accept help from other therapists, that contribution to treatment will have been a significant one.

10

A Physician's Perspective on the Interdisciplinary Management of Child Abuse

Eli H. Newberger, MD

INTRODUCTION: THE PROBLEM

The management of child abuse is always difficult; for several reasons, it is frequently impossible successfully to bring to bear the efforts of personnel from various disciplines. Among the more important limiting factors on effective interdisciplinary action to help the victims of child abuse and their families are the following:

1. *Lack of understanding by the members of one discipline of the objectives, standards, conceptual bases, and ethics of the others.* For example, physicians in hospitals often see social workers' professional activities in terms of referring patients to foster homes and carrying on the unpleasant—if necessary—day-to-day contacts with families for whom they have little time.

2. *Lack of effective communication from members of one discipline to members of another.* Possible examples include the important child-development observations that nurses frequently make which, for want of not having been heard, are ignored in the process of diagnostic formulation and decision making by social workers and physicians.

3. *Confusion as to which personnel can take what management respon-sibilities at what times.* In a hospital, for example, the doctor is accustomed to thinking that he is the boss; he alone decides when the patient is admitted or discharged—perhaps only on the basis of medical criteria. Upon the child's discharge, he may expect that the protective service's social worker will obediently knock on his patient's family's door, hat in hand, to ask, "Have you been beating your child?"

4. *Professional chauvinism.* A sense of professional pride may lead a social worker in a private family service agency to tell a colleague in a public agency or a public health nurse or physician, "Look, we've been in this business a hundred years. Who do you think you are to ask if we made a home visit last week?"

5. *Too much work for everybody, and a sense of hopelessness and despair in the face of overwhelming problems and unsympathetic colleagues.* This factor probably accounts for the large yearly turnover of social work personnel in public agencies—with the resulting loss of continuing service to individual families and of precious, experienced manpower. In Massachusetts, the staff turnover in the Division of Family and Children's Services of the Department of Public Welfare ranges up to 30% a year.

6. *Institutional relationships which limit effective inter-professional contact.* An example with which I am personally impressed is that of hospitals competing for patients and prestige. Their professional staffs (in medicine, social work, and nursing) may be reluctant to communicate with rival institutions' staffs—much less to collaborate with them in providing coordinated services to families whose individual members may receive continuing services at several clinics and offices. Social workers in public protective service programs are often isolated in state departments of public welfare. The other ancillary components of clinical child abuse management are fragmented, in most cases either into separate departments of public health or mental health or in separate private offices.

   The distinguished child psychologist Urie Bronfenbrenner has observed that American service institutions often serve to divide rather than to integrate families.[1] In child abuse management, we can often see the destructive consequences of separate institutions which attend to various aspects of welfare, health, and child development, but which cannot—because of their organization—work effectively together to strengthen family life.

7. *Prevailing punitive attitudes and public policies about child abuse.* Many professionals from outside the field turn away from involvement with protective service workers and programs as a result.

8. *A lack of confidence and trust on the part of personnel from one profession toward colleagues in the others.* This problem is made

1. Bronfenbrenner, U. *Two Worlds of Childhood.* New York: Russell Sage Foundation, 1970.

more difficult by the exceeding personal demands on everyone working with families whose children's lives are in jeopardy. The feelings within oneself generated by the anguish, remorse, anger, and guilt displayed by these families are hard to handle. They prompt serious conflicts among us and try our professionalism enormously.

9. *Cultural isolation of professional personnel.* The traditions and values of child rearing and family life among black, Spanish-speaking, or other minority families—who seem disproportionately represented in child abuse case reports—may be ignored by physicians, social workers, policemen, lawyers, and judges, who tend predominantly to be white. Because professional action on child abuse cases nearly always hinges on assessments of family competency, culture-bound value judgments can be harmful. They also promote conflict among professionals of different cultural backgrounds.

A wise and witty Supreme Court Justice, Felix Frankfurter, in his introduction to Alfred North Whitehead's book *The Aims of Education,*[2] cautioned against another, last hazard to interdisciplinary work. Concerned lest the boundaries of each professional domain be eroded in a headlong effort to foster mutual enrichment, or cross-fertilization, he warned of a possible "cross-sterilization" of the disciplines, where uncertainty in one profession would be resolved by resorting to a dubious truth in another.

In the interdisciplinary management of child abuse cases, we not infrequently fall into this trap. At the end of a difficult and frustrating case discussion, the only consensus which may be reached is "We need a psychiatric consultation," when everyone knows that the consultant's findings may only contribute further to the ambiguity and uncertainty about where to go and how to intervene. Or, also out of fear of making a management mistake, disagreeing parties conclude that the only suitable forum for discussion on conflicting perspectives is the courtroom, putting the judge in the difficult position of having to resolve conflicts among social workers and doctors and putting the family through an exceedingly stressful experience.

In the specific context in which case management takes place, a few more observations are in order.

By and large, physicians, social workers, psychiatrists, public health nurses, and legal personnel operate in relative detachment from one another. Each does what he can, often alone.

From the medical perspective, doctors often just treat the child's injury and send him on his way; psychiatrists focus on the behavior of an individual who comes to them with a proffered complaint; social

2. Whitehead, A. N. *The Aims of Education.* Mentor Book Ed. New York: New American Library of World Literature, 1949.

workers and public health nurses, who can see the family context in which child abuse occurs, may find themselves powerless to affect the actions of the other professionals with whom the family may be in contact; policemen and judges frequently apply the method most readily available to them to protect a victim of child abuse—separating the child from the parents. Each professional does what he or she can, within the ethical definition of his domain. Yet the family and its individual members can be harmed—not helped—by these well-intended, independent actions.

One is reminded of the comment attributed to the late Abraham Maslow (1908–1970) to the effect that if the only tool you have is a hammer, you tend to treat every problem as if it were a nail.

We now have several excellent studies of foster home care and its consequences; these investigations demonstrate the risks and costs of the most readily available child protective practice.

In the professional practice of child protection, we now know that with the right kind of interdisciplinary cooperation, families can be kept together and made to be safer, more nurturant contexts in which children who have suffered abuse can grow. The appearance in the last year of a landmark volume, edited by Drs. C. Henry Kempe and Ray E. Helfer, *Helping the Battered Child and His Family,*[3] heralds a new era of protective practice. Now professional energies may be invested more in the direction of making families stronger than in simply assuring that children's risk of repeated injury is reduced. It is especially encouraging to see this interest in the medical community—about a century behind the pioneers of the child welfare movement.

THE CHALLENGE OF INTERDISCIPLINARY CHILD ABUSE MANAGEMENT

We professionals in the field face an important challenge in fostering interdisciplinary cooperation and in developing effective and humane child abuse programs. I would like to present a rationale for the clinical management of child abuse in the initial crisis period when interdisciplinary cooperation is most vital.

I will consider interdisciplinary practice—admittedly and unabashedly from a physician's perspective—in the critical period when a family in crisis presents an abused child for care.

A consensus on seven axioms of child abuse management appears in child abuse literature:

---

3. Kempe, C. H. and Helfer, R. E., eds. *Helping the Battered Child and His Family.* Philadelphia: Lippincott, 1972.

1. Once diagnosed, a child with inflicted injury or neglect is at great risk for reinjury or continued neglect.

2. Protection of the child must be a principal goal of initial intervention, but protection of the child must go hand-in-hand with the development of a program to help the family through its crisis.

3. Traditional social casework in itself cannot protect a battered or neglected child in the environment in which he received his injuries. Medical follow-up, too, is necessary, and day-to-day contact with a child care center may help significantly to encourage his healthy development.

4. In the event the child is reinjured and medical attention is sought anew, it is likely that the parents or caretaker will seek care at a different facility from the one at which the diagnosis was originally established or suspected.

5. The problems of public social service agencies in both urban and rural areas—specifically in numbers of adequately trained personnel and in quality of administrative and supervisory functions—militate against their effective operation in isolation from other care-providing agencies. Simply reporting a case to the public agency mandated to receive child abuse case reports may not be sufficient to protect an abused or neglected child or to help the family.

6. Early identification by professional personnel of the immediate agent of the injury, or attempts to determine if neglect was "intentional," may be ill-advised. However strategic the "facts" may be to confirmation of diagnosis and treatment planning, clinical experience attaches the greater importance to the establishment of confidence and trust in the intervening professionals. This relationship may be jeopardized by overly aggressive attempts to elicit specific information on the circumstances of the injury. There is rarely any need to establish precisely who it was who injured or neglected a child and why. Lack of evidence for parental "guilt," furthermore, is emphatically not a criterion for discharge of the patient.

7. If there is evidence that the child is at major risk, hospitalization to allow time for assessment of his home setting is appropriate. Infants under a year of age with fractures, burns, or bruises of any kind are especially at risk for reinjury or for serious consequences of neglect. Prompt and effective intervention is vital to assure their survival.

ASSESSMENT OF THE CHILD AND HIS FAMILY

An adequate general medical history and physical examination are necessary at the time the child is brought to the physician. Photographs and a skeletal X-ray survey are performed when deemed appropriate. A social worker, if available, is called promptly at the time of the family's presentation; this contact with the family is supported by the physician, who introduces the worker as someone interested and able to help them through this difficult period and who confers with the worker after the initial interview.

In the initial interviews and in subsequent contacts, no direct or indirect attempt is made to draw out a confession from the parent. Denial is a prominent ego defense in virtually all abusing parents, and the bizarre stories often heard from them about how their children got their injuries ought not to be taken as intentional falsifications. These odd accounts often tell how profoundly distressing it is to a parent to acknowledge having inflicted an injury or having failed to protect a child from someone else's having done so. In the face of such a threatening reality, they repress it, literally to hold themselves together; they may offer blatantly phony stories, which must be accepted for the moment.

A professional does no service to parent and patient with assaults on the parent's personality structure. The third degree or its gentlemanly equivalent serves often to harden the defense or to promote more primitive defenses—resistance to talking about the problem at all, angry outbursts directed at the interviewer or at the hospital, or threats to take the child home immediately. Such defenses limit both the process of information gathering and the prospects for continuing helpful professional relationships; they may possibly endanger the child. Rather, good interview technique allows parent and child to maintain the integrity of ego and family as it is in each case. Although spoken or suggested skepticism about the proffered explanation also operates deleteriously, it is appropriate to emphasize the child's need for care—which may include his admission to a hospital—and the need to ensure that he is protected from harm. At this time, the professionals should demonstrate concern and ability to help the parent's distress as well.

In explaining his legal obligation to report the case, the physician's compassion and honesty will go far to allay the family's anxiety.

The opportunity to observe parent-child interaction and the child's physical and psychological milestones (which might yield insight into the familial causes of a child's injury) may not be available to a physician in his office. Nurses in clinical and public health settings can and do, however, make such observations, which are fundamental in casefinding and evaluation. Their competence contributes uniquely to diagnosis, and their perceptions should be shared appropriately with the physician and social worker seeing the family. A description of the child's development —perhaps augmented by a Denver Developmental Screening Test—and of his interaction with his family, is usually recorded in the nurses' notes.

A home visit by a public health nurse or social worker is made to develop a reasoned perception of the child's home environment and to gather data for the discussion of the child's disposition.

A psychiatric consultation is frequently obtained on cases of child neglect and abuse. Often this consultant's perceptions lead to understanding of what intervention by which personnel can be most effective. Only rarely, however, can a psychiatrist work magic; his consultation—always desirable but often difficult to arrange—should be a helpful adjunct to the planning process for the primary managers, social worker, physician, and nurse. Psychiatric consultation should not substitute for careful history taking and diagnostic assessment by the personnel who will continue to follow the child and his family.

The development of programs which attend to these principles will require careful thought and planning. In the last analysis, our ability to convince our patients or clients that we mean to help them depends on our ability to mobilize effective services for them. When we do so, case reports from all practitioners will certainly come easier and our ability to enlist our colleagues—some of whom are now reluctant even to report child abuse cases—in an interdisciplinary effort will improve as well.

11 Nursing Responsibility on a Child Abuse Team

Elizabeth H. McAnulty, RN

Often when people ask about my job, I am hesitant to acknowledge that I am a nurse on a child abuse treatment team; the very words imply drama and the notion that treatment of child abuse is contained within the walls of a hospital by a specialized group of professionals. I believe that a child abuse team is essential in directing, supporting, and co-ordinating the work of hospital and community persons. In truth, though, the real treatment of the problem lies with those persons in direct contact with the hospitalized child and his family and with the community persons who counsel the family long before and long after they pass through the hospital doors. Rather than drama, the work involves much frustration in reaching even limited goals; it provokes discouragement with the paucity of such community services as day care or family counselling; it requires real emotional stamina and courage in convincing other professionals of the actuality of situations which may be painful to face.

Nurses in hospitals, clinics, schools, and public health are in very strategic positions for recognizing cases of child abuse or neglect. It is therefore ironical that, until very recently, they were not legally mandated to report cases, as are doctors, social workers, and teachers. Certainly the nurse's accurate assessment and acceptance of her responsibility to aid the family and to communicate appropriately with other professionals is crucial to the early diagnosis and treatment of these troubled families. Indeed, the nurse's skilled appraisal and her sensitivity to the situation may determine the speed and efficiency of the family's entry into a system of helping structures which to them might seem hopelessly complex and threatening.

Too often nurses feel that it is the social worker's role or the job of the hospital's child abuse team to deal with the family. This attitude reflects both a wish to avoid the problem, and anger toward the family. In emergency rooms and clinic settings and on inpatient hospital units, the nursing staff has the most frequent contact with the family. In many instances, this staff can be the least threatening contact—particularly if the nurse is sensitive to the child's injury as symptomatic of pervasive deprivation and stress in the family's situation. It is most important that the nurse recognize inner feelings of anger toward the parent and desire to "rescue" the child. Often, feelings such as these are displaced onto other team members; they thwart the real goal of nurturing the parents in order that they might better nurture the child. Having team members to whom the nurse can turn for ventilation of feelings and help in objectively managing a case is essential, even if such professionals are not centrally involved.

Usually the chief areas of nursing evaluation are physical appraisal of the child, assessment of his emotional and developmental competence, and observation of the quality of parent-child interaction, the parents' level of fulfillment as adults, and the family's adaptation to strengths and weaknesses of their situation. At Children's Hospital, we have found the nurse's observations of these areas invaluable; it is most important to have the nurses on the divisions accompany rounds and come to the Trauma X conferences each week.

While the child is hospitalized, it is almost always a time of tremendous stress for the parents, and they are almost invariably mistrustful of any professionals and, subsequently, hostile. Throughout their own formative years, these parents have often been given scant basis for establishing trust in others or belief in their own self-worth. Often, the child's injury can be interpreted as an oblique plea for help—albeit pathetically desperate. It is most important for nurses dealing with the problem of child abuse to be aware of the basis for the parents' behavior. Attempts should be made to minimize the number of persons having contact with the child and with the family. The child needs to develop trust in particular persons. The family may be terribly threatened by nurses and doctors and uncertain if anyone understands them. Since the parents will rarely ask for help in interpreting the plans for the child

—and may even feel too frightened to visit—it is important for the nurse to initiate contacts with the parents.

Parents who abuse or neglect their children often have only a minimal understanding of normal child development. Frequently during the crisis associated with hospitalization, it is not feasible to do much teaching about child care. The nurse may, in nondirective ways, serve as a role model for the parents if he or she is able at the same time to meet the parents' needs for recognition and, very possibly, for dependence. On discharge, visiting nurses can be most helpful to the family; it is often helpful to introduce this person to the family before the child goes home.

Very often children who have been victims of abuse present real behavior problems; in the hospital, they may need to be subject to restrictions and physical restraints. In setting limits and planning for the placement of the child on the ward, the nurse needs to respond to the child's individuality rather than react to his overt behavior. Again, limiting as much as possible the numbers of persons interacting with the child benefits all concerned.

In summary, nurses on a multidisciplinary team can make a considerable contribution in managing cases of child abuse. It is impossible for any one profession to handle adequately the many ramifications of child abuse. Mutual dependence and trust are essential to maintaining optimum communication.

12 Role of a Child Psychiatrist as a Consultant to a Hospital Trauma Team

Alan N. Marks, MD

INTRODUCTION

Hospitals that have actively addressed abuse and neglect in children discovered early in their efforts that an interdisciplinary team approach is necessary for any degree of success in dealing with the problem.

After the group members are chosen from the professional staffs of the hospital, the process of developing a working group with defined goals is the first order of business. Only after the group works out role definition, trust, and respect can it confront the following tasks: formulate a program suitable for the population served by the hospital, implement the program, and provide continuing education to the staff of the hospital in order to insure the viability of the program.

The Tufts-New England Medical Center Hospital, Boston, Mass., developed an interdisciplinary team called Children's Advocate Group (CAG) in 1972. The team consists of members from hospital administration, including legal services, and from nursing, pediatrics, child psychiatry, and social service.

CAG meets on a weekly basis; it usually discusses five cases in a meeting. CAG functions as a consultant to the individual staff person who presents a neglect and/or trauma problem to the group. CAG attempts to utilize available resources in the hospital and/or community to implement an appropriate treatment plan for the child and family.

This brief chapter intends to introduce some of the main functions of the child psychiatrist consultant to a hospital-based trauma team.

GROUP FORMATION

Initial Phase

Individuals from the various hospital staffs joined CAG voluntarily. Presumably all members shared some common interest in the problem of abuse/neglect. In the beginning, CAG members felt close to one another until actual case material was presented. At that time, the group was characterized by fear, anger, and ambivalence. The child psychiatrist was set up to answer questions that no one could possibly answer; the group members began to feel disappointed and angry at the child psychiatrist. Factions developed which were detrimental to the efficient functioning of the group. Slowly, the child psychiatrist began to help people define their roles in the group; as role definition was catalyzed, mutual trust seemed to follow in a short period. Very few patient problems were discussed by the child psychiatrist during this initial phase.

Trust or Working Phase

During this phase, each member is aware of his or her own abilities. The child psychiatrist's role is quite flexible during this phase. For example, he can consult with a staff person or CAG member about some aspect of a case that is worrisome to that particular staff person. The patient and/or family can be seen by the child psychiatrist consultant only after some specific reasons are jointly defined by staff member and child psychiatrist.

The child psychiatrist primarily helps the members clarify the general psychiatric questions about the cases. This consultative role helps the staff put the case material in perspective so that referrals to the most appropriate agencies can be accomplished and sensible treatment plans ensue.

Regressive Phase

The optimal methodology for designing and implementing a program to identify and treat the abused/neglected child and family awaits the results of current research and demonstration projects. Many group members become quite angry when a treatment plan proves to be unsuccessful. These members may regress to the initial phase of group relatedness for a short time. With or without the help of the child psychiatrist, these members realize that their attitude is having a destructive influence on the group. After a period of brief ventilation concerning the frustrating aspects of the work, the member assumes the trusting role again. There have been no problems with members maintaining the regressed position. A new member entering the group usually makes a rapid transition through the initial phase to the trusting phase.

EVALUATION OF HOSPITAL STAFF GROUP REACTION TO ABUSE AND NEGLECT

During the initial phase of the group, there were intense struggles with angry feelings in most members—feelings often projected on to other members. The conflict that most members were defending against had to do with inability to help the individual who inflicted injury because of rage against this person.

Other members identified with the inflictor's impulsive process. This identification with agressor provided these members with an intense conflict over ability to recognize inflicted trauma or neglect in a child. Denial and avoidance were the primary defenses used by these members in their approach to the child's problems. It is very important to note that these CAG members still presented the cases to the group, but they demonstrated great discomfort when questioned about their formulation—which always denied that any direct trauma or neglect existed. Their reasons for presentation always seemed vague, so other members often questioned why cases were presented. Presumably, the members were ambivalent about their ego defenses in relation to the cases and actually desired direct confrontation to resolve the ambivalence. In no cases presented were inflicted injuries and/or neglect at issue.

As the staff members were able to talk to each other in a more open manner (trust), they talked directly about their feelings in relationship to cases. The members of CAG were able to see that effective evaluation could not be accomplished if group members acted out their personal conflicts with family or child. The child psychiatrist was active in gently pointing out these issues as the group entered the trusting phase. One year elapsed before the intense struggles over these issues subsided.

At the present time, CAG functions in an organized fashion. The group uses the child psychiatrist's skills both for consultation to member or staff person and to evaluate a patient and/or family.

PART FIVE

DIAGNOSIS AND TREATMENT

13 The Physically Abused Child

Irving Kaufman, MD

This chapter focuses on the personality factors found in the parents who physically abuse children.

This problem has been viewed in various ways. They include consideration of that point at which normal discipline becomes abuse and of how often abuse fantasies are part of the thinking of many parents who do not actually abuse their child. In addition, the frequency of the type of overtly damaging parent-child behavior depends on the setting in which it is observed. For example, by perhaps 90%, the cases seen in a protective agency will be for neglect, with about 10% referred for abuse. In the hospital setting, only those types of neglect which include malnutrition and neglect of physical health are seen; most of the other such cases would be battered children.

Marion Morris, in her discussion of child abuse,[1] places it in the framework of the normal developmental pattern of parents' relationship to children. She refers to the active process a mother goes through in

---

1. Morris, M. G., Gould, R. W., and Matthews, P. J. Toward Prevention of Child Abuse. *Children.* March–April 1974.

"claiming" a new infant. By this, she means fitting the infant into the already existing relationship between herself and father and other significant figures. This "claim" process also undoubtedly refers to the father's attitude. Both parents have to identify the baby with elements in themselves which are given a positive value. The identification, in turn, gives the parents a positive feedback, making it more possible to give the infant the positive stimuli necessary for normal emotional development. Mrs. Morris gives a detailed list of the attributes and characteristics of the parents and their interaction with the infant which produce this type of positive relationship.

She contrasts this normal pattern with the situation where the "claiming" process fails; she calls it a form of "psychological miscarriage." Under these circumstances, the parents see the child in negative terms and respond accordingly. According to this conceptualization, the parents attack the child at the point where the parents are in an "over-stressed" situation; they strike out at their child to relieve their own feelings of distress. In this role reversal, the child is seen as the attacker and the parent the victim.

Dr. Milowe [2] in his studies of child abuse referred to three issues:

1. In some families, violence can be traced through at least three generations.

2. There are indications that some batterings occur only when specific developmental stages in the child trigger specific conflicts in the parent—not at earlier or later times.

3. Cases have been reported in which the same child is battered in sequential foster homes where no other child has ever been battered. This third point raises the interesting question as to whether or not some inherent or very early acquired trait in the child may provoke the battering he receives.

There have been various attempts to clarify the types of parents who abuse children. Edgar Merrill, in his study of 115 families showing physical abuse to children seen at the Children's Protective Services,[3] discussed the characteristics of the families.

1. The majority of these families had lived in their communities for years.

2. The majority of the families were self-supporting.

3. They showed little integration in the community—few group associations.

2. Milowe, I. D. Patterns of Parental Behavior Leading to Physical Abuse of Children. Presented at workshop sponsored by the Children's Bureau in collaboration with the University of Colorado School of Medicine. Colorado Springs. March 21–22, 1966.
3. Merrill, E. J. Physical Abuse of Children—An Agency Study. Presented at the 89th annual forum of the National Conference on Social Welfare. New York City. May 31, 1962.

4. Ninety percent of these families had serious social problems such as marital discord and financial difficulty.

He described four distinct clusters of personality characteristics of both the mothers and fathers:

1. Hostility and aggressiveness—continually angry at someone or something. The anger, which stems from internal conflicts, could be stimulated by the normal difficulties usually experienced daily.

2. Rigid, compulsive parents lacking warmth, reasonableness, and pliability in their thinking and in their beliefs. They were compulsive house cleaners.

3. Parents with strong feelings of passivity and dependence—sad, moody, and immature parents.

4. A considerable number of abusing fathers. These fathers had trouble supporting their families because of physical disabilities. The mothers worked and supported the fathers who stayed home. The home atmosphere was rigid and controlled.

Mrs. Morris also described four types of parents who abuse children.[4]

1. The parent who is distressed and often guilty about the relationship and treatment of the child.

2. The undercontrolled, impulse-ridden parent who is angry about the relationship with his child and who blames him wholeheartedly for the trouble.

3. The overcontrolled parent who feels "correct" in his relationship with the child and whose actions of abuse appear more planned than the other three groups.

4. The parent who responds to inner stimuli and events rather than to the real world and the child.

Brant Steele and his group in Denver discussed the families who abuse children in terms of their severe personality problems.[5] These people were isolated from the community; they tended to see the child as the attacker against whom they had to defend themselves.

Dr. Steele and his associates stated that the common denominator of all their patients who abused children was a pattern of child rearing characterized by premature demand of high performance and

4. Morris, M. G. Maternal Claiming—Identification Processes; Their Meanings for Mother-Infant Mental Health. Presented at the 42nd annual meeting of the American Orthopsychiatric Association. New York City. March 19, 1965.
5. Steele, B. F., Pollack, C. B., and Davoren, E. Patterns of Parental Behavior Leading to Physical Abuse of Children. Presented at workshop sponsored by the Children's Bureau in collaboration with the University of Colorado School of Medicine. Colorado Springs. March 21–22, 1966.

compliance with satisfaction of parental needs. Accompanying this pattern is a complete disregard for what the infant might need and for his performance possibilities. Specifically, abusing parents do not perceive the infant as an infant but as an organized human capable of sensing their own needs and meeting them. The attacking person has grown up in a strikingly similar milieu, without having experienced this sense of being mothered. These patients feel unloved, unlistened to, uncared for, and deeply worthless. They have often been the focus of extreme concern which has taken the form of demand and attack rather than anything approximating kindness or sympathy.

Therapy with the parents has been directed toward making them aware that they are individuals with needs, feelings, thoughts, wishes —personal beings who can be recognized as such by someone other than their babies.

Treatment is directed toward the parent—recognizing his need for parenting. Dr. Steele found the mothers have given up the hope of finding the mother in a woman; they are more able initially to turn to a male therapist for the mothering they seek. Dr. Steele states that an incredible sense of aloneness and worthlessness, and a desire for the child to take care of the unheeded needs of yesterday are present. When the child does not heed, he or she is often beaten.

In the study, Dr. Steele pointed to isolation, disturbances in reality testing, extreme dependency needs, and a reversal of parent-child roles. These various descriptions deal with impulses and their controls.

Dr. Galdston of Boston Children's Hospital Medical Center [6] discussed seven factors which he felt predisposed parents to resort to the physical abuse of children in order to spare themselves the conscious experience of their own intrapsychic stress.

1. Reliance on projection as a leading defense against intrapsychic stress. A defect appears in the capacity to test the reality of the child. The child functions as a delusion, in what is essentially a transference psychosis.

2. A tendency to translate affect states into physical activity without the intervention of conscious thought.

3. The presence of intolerable self-hatred. The parent takes out this hatred on the child. The parent abuses the child for attributes which he or she cannot inwardly tolerate.

4. Correspondence of the child by sex, age, and position in the family to events in the parent's own life which occasioned the self-hatred.

5. Relative lack of available alternative modes of handling conflict because of environmental factors.

6. Gladstone, R. Observations on Children Who Have Been Physically Abused and Their Parents. *Amer. J. Psychiatry.* 122:440–444, 1965.

6. Compliance with the act of abuse by the marriage partner because of dependence and a reciprocal willingness to support projective defenses.

7. Relative absence of available authority figures in grandparents or religious or social authorities.

In his observations, Dr. Galdston pointed out that the core disturbance is a form of psychosis.

The child who is the victim of abuse not only faces real danger to life and limb, but tends to incorporate the pattern of aggressive discharge to cope with anxiety which his parents exhibit toward him. These patterns tend to be repeated from generation to generation.

The child who is attacked physically or is sexually assaulted is in a setting where the following group of problems occur in the parents:

1. Problems in control of aggressive and/or sexual impulses.

2. Problems in reality testing.

3. Problems in the superego—ranging from an unawareness of appropriateness of child care to the use of discipline as a rationale for abuse.

In general, the cases illustrate problems of impulse control—both aggressive and sexual. The abuse is not an isolated characteristic of the parent, but one of the many pathologic ways of discharging tension and coping with stress. The range of disturbance in some of the cases may include violence to children and spouse, incest, promiscuity, homosexuality, thought disorders, various psychosomatic symptoms—all of which add up to a breakdown in the capacity to manage stress. In some instances, the breakdown may be episodic and cyclical, with periods and patterns of surprisingly adequate behavior such as taking care of the house, managing a budget, and holding a job.

We know that most of these parents do not continuously beat or harm their child; they react in outbursts at times of stress. They show their other disturbances in episodic ways. This behavior creates problems in their treatment, both in evaluating where they are at any given time and in that many of them can pull themselves together and make a good appearance in such a setting as a court.

Child abuse is a reflection of an internal struggle in the parent. Although it is frequently referred to by the parent in terms of discipline, it has no real relationship to discipline. The objective of discipline is to teach the child some principle. The objective of child abuse is to cope with overwhelming tension in the parent. This differentiation appears to be true whether the episode is triggered by an overreaction to normal behavior, such as crying, or to the provocative behavior of children who manage to get abused by a series of parent figures.

The extraordinarily narcissistic orientation of abusive parents means it is necessary to focus the treatment on them. Brant Steele vividly described this process in his work with abusing parents where he had to come into the setting as the parental figure recognizing the needs of the parents. Obviously, if the child's life is in danger, protection would take first priority; to the extent that the case allows focus on the parents and their own enormous feelings of being the abused victims, he felt treatment was most promising.

Regardless of the core fantasy associated with the parent's attack upon the child, the point at which the attack occurs requires a major distortion in reality for the parent to be able to carry out a brutal assault on a child. The child is no longer perceived as helpless—dependent on his parents for love, care, and nurture—but as some symbol upon whom the assault is launched.

There are a number of fantasies upon which the parent builds up the explosive tension which leads to the battering. Some of these fantasies, listed below, have been touched on in various literary and psychiatric sources.

1. A father was beating his son unmercifully. A widower, he seemed harassed as he attempted to care for his family. The child whom he battered was the youngest, and his birth was associated with the death of his mother in childbirth. The father projected the family difficulties upon this child, whom he consciously blamed for the death of his wife and toward whom he mobilized his massive rage for her death.

2. In some cases, the child is seen as a sibling rival. For example, a father, who had become increasingly alcoholic with the birth of each child, became brutally assaultive and attacked the child he called "the champ," whom he felt was mother's favorite. This inadequate, passive-dependent man's alcoholism was an attempt to gain oral supplies in competition with his children, who were being cared for by their mother. His rage and battering of the child arose out of this competition, frustration, and sibling rivalry. In some cases, the crying of the young child and the associated oral-dependent demands will mobilize an unreasoning rage in parents who are in competition with their child for oral supplies.

3. The attack upon the child can be a sexualized assault. In some cases, the child may commit some act contrary to the parents' rules, wishes, or desires. This occasion is seized upon as a reason to mete out punishment to the child; there may well be a time delay between the child's behavior and the punishment. Characteristic of the pattern in this type of case, the beating of the child rises in intensity and the parent, with many moralistic verbalizations, justifies his or her brutality. However, at times the parent may become frightened when the beating seems to be taking over and growing in intensity and excitement. Despite the pseudo-logic behind the need to teach the child right from wrong, the parent becomes aware that his or

her behavior is getting out of control. The beatings often have an orgastic quality where the parent becomes excited, breathless, exhausted, and drained following beating of the child. In these cases, the child is utilized as a masturbatory equivalent for the discharge of sado-masochistic sexual tensions.

4. It is my impression that the most frequent instances of battering of a child occur in connection with issues of control. In practice there may be many variations on this theme.

For example, one parent phoned to say that she had beaten her child and had him tied up in the basement; would someone come over immediately before she did something to the child which she regretted. The history revealed that this was a Jewish woman, the victim of Nazi persecution and incarceration in a concentration camp. Her parents had been killed in a gas chamber, and she felt considerable guilt at being the only survivor in her family. Her assault upon her child, whom she described as incorrigible and uncontrollable, was predictable. Included were such elements as an identification with the aggressor who assaulted and destroyed her family. A part of her wanted some outside force to step in and stop the destruction.

She had to create the crisis of beating, potential murder, and rescue, to undo what had happened in her life. A lack of differentiation and a disturbance in ego boundaries occurred between her and her child. To some extent, she saw herself as victim; to another extent, she also saw the child as potential victim. The battering and the call to the agency were attempts to cope with the psychotic-like trauma of her life.

More frequent than the above example are the instances where there is an intact family, and one of the parents brutally assaults the child because the child disobeys, drops food on the floor, or appears to the parent as the aggressor controlling the parent. For example, when a small child dropped some food out of his high chair onto the immaculate floor of his parents' home, his mother grabbed him, flung him against the wall, and kicked him repeatedly, breaking several bones and causing extensive bruises. The father, hearing the noise, rushed in and stopped the assault. The child was hospitalized. However, the father was very supportive of the mother; he saw the child as difficult to manage. In the interim between such attacks, the child was well fed, and received adequate medical care and affection from both parents.

In this type of case, the parents' emotional structure is in a delicate balance. They are in a symbiotic tie with the child. The child's "naughty" behavior threatens to upset this delicate balance, and the parent fears loss of control, weakening ego overwhelmed by massive anxiety, and self-destruction. To protect himself or herself, the parent attacks the child.

This type of case represents an episodic type of psychosis where the parent's attack is a last desperate attempt to protect himself or herself against the dissolution of his or her own ego.

5. Battering associated with gross psychosis, which also takes various forms. In postpartum psychosis, one of the most frequent fears,

phobias, anxieties, and sometimes behavior, is the fear that the mother will destroy her child. In some cases where the parent has a paranoid psychosis, the child—caught up in the delusional system—becomes the object of the parent's aggressive attention. This may take various bizarre forms such as locking the child in a closet, chaining him to a bed, beating him, or starving him to death.

6. In a few instances the parents, in a cold, calculating way, obtain insurance on the life of the child or children, and systematically batter them until they die; the parents then collect on the insurance.

Treatment and management of the various types of battering of children by parents require an understanding of the reason for the battering in order to be able to apply the appropriate remedial measures.

Protective casework service reflects an attempt on the part of the community to deal with a serious deficiency in one of the fundamental components of our society—disturbance or inadequacy of child rearing. Dr. Leontine Young stresses the importance of diagnosis as the only means to determine possible goals before effective work can be done with the families.[7] Generally speaking, the protective caseworker enters when the deviation is so gross and extreme that it cannot be ignored. Ideally, two major departures from this established norm would occur: (1) an earlier detection of cases before they became so advanced and (2) a finding of cases in their less extreme forms, which probably are amenable to more successful intervention.

In summary, a group of parents who abuse their children reveal a disturbance in their reality testing. They show a reversal in parent-child roles and perceive their child as big and powerful and themselves as weak and helpless. At times of stress, they develop an episodic psychosis and attack their child out of the delusion that they are protecting themselves from being destroyed. Intensive casework focusing on the parents as the prime clients is essential if work with the families is to be possible. It is necessary to evaluate those situations where the parental pathology is so severe that real danger exists for the child and the child must be removed. However, the intense hostile tie between parents and child often leads to paradoxical behavior. For example, placement of an abused child in a loving home setting may not work because the child runs to his abusing parents. Generally, it is desirable to deal not only with the disturbance in the parent-child pathology but also with the internalized disturbance in the abused child.

---

7. Young, L. R. The Behavior Syndromes of Parents Who Neglect and Abuse their Children. Ph.D. dissertation, School of Social Work, Columbia University, 1963.

14 Viewing Child Abuse and Neglect as Symptoms of Family Dysfunctioning

Nancy C. Avery, ACSW

The treatment goal in protective service is to strengthen the family unit by helping the parents deal with unresolved conflicts, feelings of inadequacy, loneliness, and/or a lack of confidence—thereby enhancing their capacity and ability to provide good child care. The appropriate treatment method is arrived at by evaluating the family on two levels— the individual interpersonal, and the family dynamic—always with an awareness of the vulnerability of the child in his environment. I will discuss intervention and treatment in terms of these two levels of dysfunction.

One of the first and most difficult things the therapist must do is to deal with his or her own feelings about a parent who has hurt a small child. Most people react with disbelief or denial or, on the other hand, with horror and anger toward the abuser. To be effective, we must attain a neutralized position. We are not treating symptoms; we are treating total people who may be hurt children themselves.

Facing society's attitudes—and our own feelings—may help us to understand the different ways families present themselves upon the initiation of service. Depending on the parents' past experience with authority figures, they may react in one of two completely divergent manners. One father may angrily insist that there are no problems in his home, he doesn't need any help, and the social worker should be over in the neighborhoods where people really need help. Another parent may passively nod, indicating a willingness to cooperate. Of course, most reactions are a combination of these two. No matter how the parents present themselves, their expectations are that they will be used, attacked, and accused of being "bad" parents. In fact, these parents may have been talked to in an accusatory manner by other helping persons. A single statement to indicate understanding—that the parents have been having a tough time—lets them know immediately that you are different and that you are interested in them and how they feel. The helping process has begun if we can get parents to talk about their frustrations and problems.

The greatest barrier to developing a trusting relationship is a fear of rejection or abandonment. These parents feel that if they begin to trust and risk exposing themselves, the therapist will see how truly unworthy of being liked they are and will desert them. This imagined or exaggerated feeling of being rejected by the worker is often the reason why parents break away from treatment. Breaking away may happen after the parent has exposed himself during a time of crisis.

A mother called me late one afternoon, crying hysterically. It was impossible for me to discern what had happened to make her so upset. It was the tone of my voice and not what I said that eventually quieted her down. Very upset with the actions of her child, this mother called me rather than lashing out at the child. Our contact had clearly been set around abuse of one child, but she had never before exposed her angry, impulsive feelings; she avoided me for a few weeks thereafter. In helping her deal with this crisis situation, I had not addressed her feelings. The fact that this child's actions may have made her look like a bad mother in the neighborhood made her uncertain of how I saw her. Misunderstandings must be discussed openly. The parents' nagging sense of inferiority is diminished with reassurance that the worker accepts them with all their limitations.

Some parents have a difficult time allowing anyone to get close; just when you feel the relationship is beginning to gel, they reject you. When the conflict arises between the desire for a close relationship with you and the fear that you may hurt or desert them, you, the worker become the good parent. These parents have experienced a deprivation of basic mothering—a lack of early awareness that someone cared for them and cared about them. They were never seen as children or as individuals with needs, desires, worth, and potential. They were subjected to excessive demands for performance beyond their maturational abilities and to severe criticism. No matter what the child tried to do, it did not meet with parental approval.

These parents have little self-esteem to carry them through stressful periods. These parents, like their parents before them, turn to their children for their own emotional satisfaction. The child unable to meet parental expectation is punished excessively. The social worker, as the good parent, fosters a corrective experience to reverse this pattern of unmet needs. As parents are allowed to become dependent on the worker —and have their own needs met—they are able to respond more appropriately to their own children. The social worker must be comfortable with allowing dependency. We cannot expect these parents to stand on their own two feet and be responsible, because they have experienced this expectation all their lives with no recognition of their legitimate needs.

Delores—a mother of two children, Billy, age 4, and Agnes, age 3—experienced severe maternal deprivation. She was shuffled from foster home to foster home. Delores thought she was moved because she misbehaved. In one foster home, she and the other foster children were treated as outcasts and separated from the rest of the family. It is no wonder that this mother sees herself as beneath others—as worthless and unlovable. As a teenager, she was removed from foster care to take care of her alcoholic mother. When she met her husband, Frank, 18, they married almost immediately to give each other a home. Frank's parenting was also poor because both of his parents were alcoholics. Frank simply did not know how to give Delores the nurturing and loving care for which she turned to him.

When Agnes was born, Frank began to run around with other women. Mother became extremely depressed and paid little attention to the new baby. At 9 months, Agnes was admitted to the hospital with the diagnosis of failure to thrive. The child had not received affection, was listless, and had severe urine burns. Mother neglected Agnes the way she perceived she was treated as a child. She turned to Billy for the love and affection she never got. Mother was permissive with Billy and over-punitive toward Agnes.

Mother was isolated, lonely, and mistrustful of the world outside her small apartment, so the social worker concentrated on her. Initially, they got out of the house together—a walk to the store and a cup of coffee on the way back. Mother began to dress up for these outings, responding to the worker's positive support. At the same time, the worker began to use herself as a model to involve the outcast child in the family. As Agnes began to develop, it became visible proof to this mother that she was doing a good job.

It has taken Delores two years to acknowledge that the worker is the only person who really cares about her and to risk letting the worker know how much she has invested in their relationship. They have moved in treatment to the issues around her hostile/dependent relationship with her mother, feelings of grief for her father, and the self-destructive patterns of behavior she has tried to use to fill the emptiness inside. The worker has brought a case aide into the home with her to work with the children because of their intense anxiety about possible separation from their mother.

We can generalize about descriptive characteristics of abusing families, but it is not the whole story. Emotional disturbance may fall anywhere on the continuum from psychotic to neurotic. Many other psychological and family dynamic factors should also be considered.

For example, sibling rivalry is apparent in many cases. Billy has been physically hostile toward Agnes, acting out mother's angry impulses, which she has expressed in the past with passive disinterest.

Mother has a strong need to maintain the status quo. Even though Father constantly belittles her, she is unable to leave him. She turns to her son, with whom she sleeps for the emotional gratification she never got from her father, who died when she was eight. Mother is unable to discipline her son for fear that he will reject her like the rest of the men in her life.

Another psychological factor—that of the obsessive-compulsive personality traits—offers important considerations for treatment. The parent requires such rigid adherence to neatness, cleanliness, and orderliness that the child cannot comply; noncompliance arouses parental wrath. If the child conforms to such expectations, he becomes a robot in his own home. If one child in the family takes on a special meaning, because he looks like someone whom the parent disliked or if the parent projects the bad side of himself onto the child, the parent may misperceive this child's actions or deeds as personal attacks or as not fitting the mold in the family constellation. The child's behavior threatens to unleash the parent's own unacceptable impulses to be messy. At an early age, the parents' needs for comfort from their parents were frustrated and unfulfilled.

The parent felt anger and aggression toward this all-powerful mother figure, but at the same time identified with this person. They perceived their behavior, which the mother figure constantly found fault with, as bad behavior; in fact, it may have been the normal exploring or crying of a small child. Having introjected their mother's feelings about their behavior, they felt guilty for the anger at the mother figure and turned the anger toward themselves. When the parent projects onto his child the badness he as a small child internalized, then he can turn the full force of the anger toward that child.

Karen's father died when she was four years old. Her six-year-old brother died when she was five years old. They had both suffered long illnesses in the home. Karen had to conform to her mother's rigid rules for a quiet household. Her mother's attention was focused on nursing the sick. Unable always to conform, Karen was made to feel responsible for their deaths.

Karen's middle child, Terry, was born at a time of financial stress and marital discord. As she became a toddler, Terry looked very much like her mother, in contrast to the other two children in the family. Mother projected her badness onto this child and singled her out for verbal abuse and criticism. Physical abuse occurred only when her husband, Harry, would desert her emotionally or physically, recreating the losses in her childhood.

Harry had an alcoholic father and an overindulgent mother, who hid all of his misdeeds from his father and allowed him to do as he pleased. He never learned to accept responsibility, but simply had a good time. He felt a strong sense of entitlement to what he wanted, when he wanted it. While Karen was overpunitive, Harry was indecisive and passive. Harry was very fond of this child and Karen was envious of the attention he showed the child. Terry became the scapegoat for parental conflicts. Harry, though not abusing, was contributing by his behavior and was passively condoning the abuse while in the home.

Getting behind these parents' projections and denials is difficult. Initially, the worker may have to focus on the child as the source of irritation and cause of the parents' difficulties. At times, the mother cannot share the worker with her husband. Her own needs are too great. However, in the situation above, father was involved in treatment around mother's anger at his gambling and lack of consistent financial and caring support of her. The focus of treatment was on the total family—not just the marital relationship.

This focus was most important because the healthy children in a family are often guilty about their actions which support the family pathology. In this case, helping father become a more active, responsible family member helped swing the balance and eventually allowed mother to look at how she felt when deserted by her husband—which really precipitated abuse rather than what the child had done.

In working with these parents, it is important to remember that they do love their children; they do not want to hurt them. They are like everyone else—they want to be received by a kind word and to be treated as if what they think and feel really matters. What may look like a dismal situation at first may turn out to be a very rewarding experience for worker and parent alike.

15 Treatment of Abusive Parents

Ann L. Arvanian,
ACSW

In planning for this chapter and in thinking over the various child-abusing families I've treated, I found myself overwhelmed with attempting to choose cases that were "typical." In reality, there is no typical case. Child abuse may be seen in conjunction with many other emotional problems; it may also occur where child abuse is the only problem. It may occur in families where neglect is also present and in families where the child's material needs are very well met. I finally narrowed my cases down to three which illustrate various treatment techniques.

In the first family, an unmarried mother, supported by welfare, had her first child, a son. The child was severely battered by the mother's boyfriend, and had to be hospitalized. X-rays revealed healed bone fractures, indicating that this child had been previously battered. In confronting the mother with this diagnosis, a skillful hospital worker felt that this mother might benefit from treatment, so I was called to meet with the mother and the hospital social worker, to talk with them about planning. Early involvement at the time of the crisis situation facilitates the therapeutic relationship. The mother readily admitted that she felt overwhelmed with the care of this child, denied ever battering him herself, but said that her boyfriend had probably done it while she was out. Actually, this explanation seemed correct.

Initially, my focus was on her life situation: What was troubling her at this time? Did she feel unloved by her boyfriend? What was her relationship with her family? How tied down did she feel with this baby? To align oneself with the parent is really the first step to be taken; the initial approach should not dwell entirely on what has happened to the child. True, the facts should be ascertained, but then the social worker should address to the parents' needs. The establishment of this therapeutic relationship is very important; it will be the main factor that prevents a rebattering. One way I overcome my personal dislike for the way the parent has treated a child—or has allowed a child to be treated —is to view the parent as a child, or a very childlike adult, who also was probably abused as a child. One of the other interesting features about this case is that mother's boyfriend had beaten her also—an action which often occurs in an abusive situation.

The treatment person should keep in mind that it is not essential to find out which parent actually did the battering. A man or woman will choose a mate to meet his or her special needs and will constantly, without treatment, continue choosing a similar mate. Also, we should not be misled when one parent requests help for the other, stating that the other parent injures or beats the child severely. In at least two of my cases, the fathers requested help due to their wives severely beating the children. In both cases, although this was so, it turned out that the father was just as harsh on the children. Treatment should keep in mind all persons within the family.

In this case, the woman needed to choose a mate who beat her and battered her child. Although she broke up with this boyfriend, her second boyfriend would probably do the same, unless she were able to choose a different type of man. Actually, she had the feeling that she was worthless and that a child of hers was probably worthless. What was needed was to improve her self-esteem. In a relationship with a helping person, she can be allowed to be dependent and have someone feel that she is worthwhile and give to her. I often call this a "reparenting." The helping person must be truly able to empathize and honestly feel for this individual. With this particular woman, we arranged to place her child in a foster home. The mother and I met weekly in her home, or sometimes we would go out for coffee and a sandwich. With the most deprived persons, taking them out to lunch or bringing presents of food is invaluable, especially when you've having difficulty in establishing the relationship. The mother and I drove the child out to the foster home and arranged for her to visit every other week at the foster home.

In the weekly talks with mother, the focus was on her. Although we talked of the child, such conversation was very brief. Treatment of this mother was based primarily on our relationship. As I gave to her emotionally, she began to identify with me; her self-esteem rose. If I saw her as having this much worth, she reasoned that she was not as worthless as she had felt. Another way I was active with her was in reuniting her with her family. Having a child out of wedlock had alienated her from her parents and siblings, and she had felt abandoned. At least half a dozen times, I met with her, her parents, and her siblings together to discuss the situation. They began to understand one another and their relationship improved. Also, I helped steer the mother to other community resources to help her with housing and health care. It is often so hard for such emotionally deprived persons to work up the courage even to use the existing community resources; they need someone to take them for the first few times. In this instance, the helping person simply acts as catalyst.

At one time in the course of treatment, she acknowledged that she had wanted to have her boyfriend beat the child and that she had done so once herself. After about four months, she started taking better care of herself, buying clothes, and talked about wanting to have her child with her. In the foster home, the child had thrived; with the longed-for attention, he emerged as a delightful, beautiful baby. During the visits at the foster home, the mother would observe the way in which the foster mother cared for the child; she actually would change his diapers in imitation of the foster mother. Initially, the child did more changing emotionally than the mother.

After about six months of treatment, the mother started to take the child to her new apartment for visits. She also, at this time, had a new boyfriend who was very different from the previous boyfriend—he wanted to marry her, bought her presents, treated her well. Within a year after the abuse, the child had been returned home for good to a considerably changed mother. A year's treatment is really very short-term in an abuse case, but this case was uncomplicated by other factors, like alcohol or psychotic behavior. Both mother and child had a mutually enjoyable relationship; they gave to each other. The child's change was important also because it helped trigger a loving response from the mother.

The second family I've chosen to discuss presents a different picture: a lovely residential neighborhood where all the homes and grounds are well kept, where a two-parent family of well-dressed, clean, church-goers lives, and three children attend school, receiving straight A's. A fourth child, a two-year-old, was at home. The referral to our agency came from a relative stating that the mother in this family was "crazy" and that the children were being tortured. I wrote to the family, stating that I'd be out at a certain time, as it had come to our attention that there were family problems. The parents were awaiting me with the children in their rooms, except for the two-year-old who was with the parents. The three older children were from the father's first marriage where his wife was deceased; the youngest child was a product of the present marriage. Neither parent denied the difficulties but expressed massive anger toward the relatives who had referred them to us, saying that the relatives had never offered any help themselves.

The mother saw me as her rescuer, saying that these children had been torturing her—that her actions toward them had only been retaliatory. There had been severe batterings, as well as some psychotic behavior toward the children. Incidentally, although the father appeared passive, he also battered the children when his wife was upset. Later in treatment, it came to light that both parents had been emotionally and physically abused as children.

This family is not as easily visible to the public as some poorer families are; those people who might have suspected family difficulties shut their eyes to it. The situation had been going on for many years, and the family relationship pattern was well established. One time the parents had tried to talk to a priest about it, but he apparently didn't want to listen. A family doctor didn't want to become involved. When the children were injured, they were simply kept out of school until the injuries healed. The parents felt relief that someone had finally found out.

From the onset, the parents entered a relationship with me. Both parents showed evidence of schizophrenia, with the child abuse being their most outstanding symptom. After the first few meetings, the parents and the children of the first marriage agreed that the mutual hatred had gone on for so many years that they would be happier with relatives; they were placed without court involvement. The stepmother had confessed that she felt so out of control at times, she thought she or their father might kill them. This situation again emphasizes the need for treatment of both marital partners. Occasionally, one parent will trigger the partner to abuse the child and never engage in such behavior. In this family, the father acted in response to his wife, battering when his wife was upset. The one child from this marriage was viewed with more positive feelings, so she remained in the home. (One danger—and a very important one—can occur when children are removed and the parents do not receive treatment. Although the removed children are considered "safe," the parents may seek replacement of them by having more children.)

Treatment consisted of weekly home visits with mother. The father and mother were seen together every few weeks in the evenings (after his work). As treatment progressed, I included the child in the latter part of our interviews—a play session. For the first hour, the mother and I would talk; for another half hour, all three of us would play ball or games together. This was a new and rewarding experience for both mother and child. One danger in this method is that the helping person might focus too much on the child and thus endanger the alignment with the parent. Other useful family activities can be used—taking parents and children to the zoo or museum.

The parents entered into an extremely dependent relationship. They had no close friends and only emotionally unstable relatives. My weekly visits assumed tremendous importance to them, and any cancellation or change in visiting time triggered a crisis. Right after placement of the other children, it emerged that the remaining child had become the focus of all the parents' anger. Although the parents could now restrain themselves from lashing out, there were occasional slips—for example, the parent pushing the child so hard that she fell, injuring herself. We focused treatment on discussion about at whom the parents were really angry—for example, their own parents—and delved into their past lives. As treatment progressed, the mother told me she had been about to hit the child; my face flashed in front of her, cautioning her to hold on a minute and think of what she was doing and with whom she was angry. This vision stopped her behavior. From that point on, internalization began; she could keep herself in check. After six months of treatment, both parents agreed that the father wasn't changing as rapidly as the mother. It was decided to see him separately, every other week in my office, so that he might focus more on his own difficulties.

After about one year in treatment, the home situation had improved, but the family faced a crisis. I was going on vacation. They panicked and said they couldn't cope with the child during this time and felt they would injure her. We must listen very carefully to what these parents tell us; if they tell us that the child must be removed, we had better pay attention. Some parents are less verbal, so they will try to tell us, via the child; for example, we start noticing bruises. Often the parent calls attention to them, saying the child had an accident. We must pay heed when parents want constant reassurance that we will not remove a child. Often this is not a fear of the parent, but a wish to have the child removed; at times, it is a necessity. During this crisis which I precipitated, the child was placed in foster care for the duration of my vacation. Any crisis can trigger abusive parents into action at times during treatment; one of the worst crises for them occurs during a loss situation. This consideration is also important when transferring the case to someone else for any reason.

Following my vacation, the child was returned. Because of the emotional pain she had felt at this unexpected separation—a terribly painful experience which sometimes causes children as much emotional pain as the battering causes physical pain—we decided to assign a social worker to work with her directly. I introduced the child's therapist

—another social worker from my agency—and thereby aligned the new worker with me. We arranged to have the mother, child, child's worker, and myself share refreshments at the kitchen table for the first 20 minutes; then the child and her worker would go into another room, and the mother and I would stay in the kitchen. When the client has such an emotional dependence on the worker, sharing the case with a co-therapist is extremely helpful to the therapist. Another reason for assigning the child a therapist stemmed from the fact that the child had learned a certain way of acting with her parents; she was having difficulty changing these responses. Often a child incorporates the parents' image of himself or herself, perceiving himself or herself as "bad." He or she feels a need to be punished and therefore may provoke caretaking persons to punish or mistreat him or may precipitate accidents to himself. Repeated accidental poisonings sometimes characterize these children—they deliberately ingest poison.

After two years of treatment, the family in this case is totally changed. They now have friends in the neighborhood; they are more trusting of persons in general; they feel pleased and happy with themselves. A more realistic view of the situation with the stepchildren is held; some visiting and some attempts at establishing a friendly relationship have occurred with the children. The larger family recognizes and is delighted by their change. The therapist should never feel hesitant about praising any change in families or reviewing progress made with them, so they can feel a sense of pride in their accomplishements. The child still within the family appears bright, lively, and happy. The parents are now learning to enjoy with their child activities that they missed as children; child and parents mutually enjoy each other. In this still continuing case, intensive, long-term, in-depth casework has provided remarkable changes.

The third family I want to discuss with you is one where both parents had a history of alcoholism and early separation from one parent; the father had been abused when he was a child. This family has multiple emotional problems, but it is also a two-parent family, not on welfare, in which the father has held down a steady job and the parents have strong somewhat rigid religious values. The referral came from a relative. This family is composed of the two parents and three children—an elder daughter and two sons. The first-born son—named after the father—was the abused child. The specific incident involved the child's playing with matches, the parents, wanting to teach him this was wrong, held his hands over the flame of the gas burner—held them too close—and the child's hands thus were burned. The child was not taken to a hospital, but simply kept home from school until his hands had healed. It evolved that there had been other abuse of this child.

In looking over past agency records, we found a case of this father's father, the paternal grandfather. The paternal grandfather had treated his son in the same manner, including the hand-burning incident, 30 years ago. Further, the record named the paternal great-grandfather as a child abuser—making it three known generations of child abuse. This generational problem is seen often in cases. Each family chooses a specific child within it—or sometimes all the children, depending on the parents' needs—to abuse. A child singled out for abuse can be either the most disliked or the most loved. Just removing the scapegoat child from the family often transfers the abuse to another child.

After sending a letter to the parents, I made the first visit. They welcomed me, saying that they wanted help and had inquired of the various agencies, but they couldn't afford to pay for psychiatric help and didn't know where else to go. Both parents were isolated people who drank alone—the father at bars and the mother at home. All of their relatives had their own problems, and there was no close friends.

The isolation of most abusing parents is really extreme. The most flagrant example that I've seen was observable in another abusing mother. She had just painted her apartment black with purple accessories, and we sat in her apartment—with the mother curled up ball-like while we talked—with no lights on. She said the apartment reflected the way she felt. Home visiting is vitally important. Most of these parents are fearful of leaving their apartments unless they go to the school, church, or store. Coming to an agency, the complications that they must face or that they fear they must face when seeking help are often too much, so an outreach approach to them is invaluable.

The family with the generational problems was willing to talk about the hand-burning incident, but they felt this was an appropriate way to teach children. The mother never took part in abusing the child or children, but she verbally agreed that they needed the discipline from the father. She was very lenient with them to make up for the father's harshness. She set no limits on their behavior at all; when the father came home at night, he felt it necessary to make up for her leniency by being extra "strict."

With most new cases the parents feel immediately that we are there to remove the children and that we are accusing them of being bad parents. Although they need reassurance that they care about their children, the worker should never make the mistake of promising that the children won't be removed. The worker must be honest, but gentle in his or her honesty—for example, saying, "Yes, I have removed children, but not often—and it doesn't seem that this is what is needed here."

For many months, I worked with this family around their problems, but their alcoholism was progressing. They enjoyed my understanding, but it didn't help them straighten themselves out. Finally, the father started beating the mother, and I realized that they were asking me for another kind of help. At this time, I told the parents I would have to go to court to ask for the removal of the children for their protection (because no relatives could take them, and the parents could not voluntarily agree to placement). When this placement occurred, the parents were relieved, although the children interpreted the foster home placement as punishment because they were bad. The child who received the brunt of the abuse became depressed; he did not really become involved with the foster parents. I remained sympathetic to the parents, but set up strict expectations for them—specifically that they would involve themselves in an alcohol treatment program. The following day I took them to the hospital alcoholic clinic. With the involvement of the clinic, they then used the AA program. Also, they now had, besides myself, another social worker from the Department of Public Welfare; this worker supervised the foster home and supervised their visiting the children. The mother then became involved in a mother's group within our agency. The most important thing with this particular family seemed to be using the authority of the court at the right time.

With this family, I saw the husband and wife together weekly on a day that the husband was off from work. This family was not able to use in-depth casework, as did the previous family discussed. For this family, we dealt with the day-to-day problems—the father's job, appropriate discipline for the children (or limit-setting, as I call it), money problems, the here-and-now. We did discuss some of their past, but not in depth. It was important for both these parents to recognize at whom they were really angry. The children have now been home a year, the parents sober for the most part, and things are going more smoothly. The children's emotional problems seemed to have eased somewhat with their parents' improvement. However, when the case was finally closed at court, the parents became fearful that they would lose my support —urging me to stay involved. This extremely dependent family will need to have supportive help from someone for many years. The pathology in their backgrounds is so severe and encompassing that it will take that long before they can give up their dependency. With this continuing support, they are functioning well, the children are happy, well taken care of, and not abused. The scapegoat child is no longer singled out in our conversations; the parents now see the children equally.

In summary, we must look at the family unit of functioning and include all members in a treatment plan. We should not be fearful of the dependent relationship that the clients enter into, but accept it as a need of the clients. Often, sharing the case with collateral agencies and workers helps with this; these families can use more than just one helping person or agency, but may have to be helped to use other community resources.

Remember that the techniques of treatment are not new; they are the regular social work tools. Emphasize caring about and acceptance of these isolated, depressed, people who feel so worthless. Primarily, our tool is the therapeutic relationship between parent and helping person. The therapist becomes the parents' parent; through identification with the therapist—as a loving, caring parent—parenting of their own children is learned. Listen and try to help them sort out their feelings—at whom they're really angry, how to love, and how to set limits for their children. But listen hard, so that if they tell you, by actions or words, that they need their children out of the home, you are prepared to take them out. In other words, constantly re-evaluate the situation.

Although these are often tremendously resistant parents, they can, with very few exceptions, use the relationship; they are capable of much change in the way they behave and relate to their children, so they are extremely rewarding persons to work with (even though it takes a long time). Just keep in mind that we can't change everything in the families. We must set realistic goals for ourselves and the families.

16 Treatment of Families in Protective Services

Nancy C. Avery ACSW

Initiating service to a family who has been referred to a protective agency, providing direct service to parents who neglect or abuse their children, is no easy job. After receiving a letter indicating that certain problems existing within the family may be affecting their children, the client's response may be one of open hostility or of passive resistance. On many occasions I have picked up the phone to hear an angry, tense voice demand to know what "this" letter is all about, quickly adding that he or she never neglects or abuses the children and that there is absolutely no need for me to visit. On many other occasions, my knocks and my one-sided conversations through closed doors have been met by silence.

Almost all parents express resentment and fear at what they feel is criticism. Often these feelings are directed at the caseworker. To be effective, the caseworker cannot take on the judgmental attitude of the community; he or she must present the community values in a way in which the therapeutic process can begin. These parents are extremely vulnerable to criticism, and they often already feel rejected. The caseworker has to find that delicate balance between presenting the referral in a straightforward, honest manner and treading softly on sensitive areas.

Any hint that you feel that these parents are inadequate can jeopardize intervention. We are not detectives; who did it is not important. What is important is that we are caring people who are concerned about their feelings and we want to help. It is our consistent caring which enables the client to enter into a relationship. The treatment which takes place within this relationship is focused on helping the parents feel more adequate and ensuring protection of the children.

A perceptive, in-depth understanding of a family is necessary before the caseworker can map out a treatment plan. The families known to protective agencies are not all alike; they come from all socio-economic levels. The psychiatric diagnoses cut the continuum from neurotic to psychotic. Characteristic typologies of families seen in protective settings are important, however, to look at and use as a backdrop in approaching and understanding a situation.

Many of these parents have never matured to adulthood; instead, they are still childlike and are trying to meet their own infantile needs. The parenting role was not pre-formed in their homes. They were never seen as people with real potential worth. Consequently, they see themselves as inadequate. Feeling insecure, they are vulnerable to criticism and they may fear abandonment. These parents have so many unmet needs that they may turn at times of crisis to their children with exaggerated demands for gratification. Since their own needs are so overwhelming and unmet, they can become angry with a child's ordinary demands. They may react by using physical force to ensure a child's proper behavior and to maintain control of a situation, or they may neglect to meet a child's everyday needs.

These parents have little ability to communicate with each other or to understand each other's needs—let alone begin to meet them. Often they communicate through a child or displace their anger and frustration with each other onto a child. These families often isolate themselves from the mainstream of society, perhaps because their demanding, controlling, destructive patterns of interaction meet with disapproval.

Emotional deprivation has retarded the maturing process. This retardation affects the interpsychic relationship, the marital relationship, the parent-child relationship, and the relationship of this disturbed family to the community. In treating these difficult and complex families, the worker takes on many roles. One worker cannot wear all the hats at once. It may be necessary for representatives of two or more agencies to combine their skills in a process of cooperative treatment. Often people from several disciplines become involved.

The challenging job for the worker is to find the correct mode of treatment and to operationalize it by integrating the many therapeutic roles into one consistent treatment plan. The modes of treatment are set up when the caseworker has established a relationship with the client; together, they have determined goals. In the protective setting, casework has been the traditional mode of treatment, with group work now being used more frequently. Within these broad structures, the worker may take on the role of enabler, advocate, ego, superego, referent to the appropriate community resource, coordinator, etc. To look at the treatment process and these different roles, I would like to present two families.

Mrs. White had a stormy marriage to her alcoholic husband. They communicated with closed fists. He died of cirrhosis of the liver two years ago. Mrs. White was an only child who escaped from caring for a bedridden mother by marrying. She remained hostilely dependent upon her father until his death six months after her husband's. After her father's death, Mrs. White began staying away for days at a time with a boyfriend. The six children were taken in by a relative, who made a referral to our agency. Prior to our involvement, the two oldest children (19 and 21) moved away from the home with angry feelings; now they rarely communicate with their mother.

Mrs. White is an orally depressed mother who is obese, spends most of her day in bed, and talks about ending it all. She at times has no control over her anger. Mrs. White's depression is based on the absence of a satisfactory parent-child relationship in her own life.

Since the worker's involvement, this mother has brought her family and her boyfriend together under one roof. Injured in World War II, he has not worked since; he spends most of his day in bed watching TV. The first few months of working with Mrs. White were spent talking about the everyday problems with which she had to cope—for example, budgeting, planning meals, or deciding on realistic but positive methods of discipline for the children. Following the initial period of relating to the basic reality problems, there was a long period of testing out. This client continually sought reassurance that her children were not going to be taken away. She also tested the worker to see if she would get a judgmental reaction about having a boyfriend live with her.

This mother had a great deal of difficulty trusting the worker; it was only after many months that she could share her true feelings about her fourth child. Vera, a 12-year-old, is named after her mother; she also has an overweight problem and wets her bed every night. The presence of a special kind of unhealthy interaction with a specific child is not uncommon. Mother identifies her child with a rejected part of herself and with her husband whom she grew to hate. Vera is acting out the bad her mother sees, which her mother unconsciously provokes.

A trusting relationship does not mean that things go along smoothly. This mother is beset by crisis after crisis. While working on a regular basis with mother, the caseworker placed Vera in a preadolescent girls' group run by another social worker in our agency. The purpose for this child is to help her deal with fear and anxiety and hostility. Much of her fear and anxiety is based on the reality threats which her mother makes. The hostility relates to her sense of deprivation and of being treated differently than the other children. Mrs. White continually makes this child feel that she gets what she deserves.

Within the group, Vera is learning that there are other children who have similar problems and feel like she does about their families. The worker lets these children know that they can be liked even with all of their "bad" feelings and that when limits and controls are imposed by the group or the leader, they are not punishment. Vera must be protected from her own self-pity—her "poor me" attitude. She must be helped to look at the fact that her mother is not a bad parent, but needs help because she never had a good parenting relationship herself. This growth includes learning that she can select those qualities from her parents which are to her advantage and incorporate other qualities from other sources. Hopefully, within this group Vera has begun to construct a new definition of herself.

Another case example using different modes of treatment is the Heath family, who was referred by a minister. He had seen these parents for marriage counseling at the request of the paternal grandmother. At the time of the referral, the mother had invited her boyfriend to live in their home, and the father had invited his girlfriend and her two children. The house in which they were living had three and one-half rooms. Neighbors reported bruises and burns on the face and neck of the Heath's only child, Robert. In a nursery school class at age six and one-half, Bobbie was showing hyperactive, sadistic, destructive behavior.

The first step in this case was to find separate living situations for these adults. The worker went in with respect for these individuals but with a firm position that their situation was destructive not only to their children, but to themselves. These parents were not happy with their living arrangements. The use of authority was a demonstration of caring and proof to these individuals that they were worthy of a better situation. With the help of the paternal grandmother, who had real estate connections in the community, all of these adults were relocated in six months. Mrs. Heath had filed for divorce, and they were preparing to sell their home.

Shortly after the worker's intervention the nursery school refused to continue with Bobbie; they could not control him. Bobbie is a child who pushes until he gets the negative response with which he is so familiar. Through the referring minister, the worker found a woman in the community to provide foster day care three days a week. This care was a great help to Mrs. Heath, who had been physically ill under the emotional strain of acting out the sado-masochistic relationship with her husband. This resource was also a godsend for Bobbie. Mrs. Fisher is a soft-spoken, patient mother of three, in the process of getting a B.A. in special education. She spent many long hours increasing Bobbie's attention span and his academic skills through creative educational aids she developed. He was able to respond to her positive, giving approach and to her consistent limit setting. Mrs. Fisher shared with Mrs. Heath, who was eager to learn from her.

At the same time, Bobbie was seeing a therapist from a local guidance clinic in a play therapy setting in preparation for public schooling. The worker became coordinator for foster day care, the psychologist, and the mother. This role is particularly important in this case because heretofore all those in the community who had contact with Bobbie reported back to his grandmother—a situation which increased the mother's feelings of inadequacy. The mother was very pleased when these people began calling her directly; she was even prouder to begin initiating contact with the school. She has made many concrete changes and has felt rewarded not only with new personal relationships, but by her immediate family. When she moved into her new apartment, her mother and sister made slipcovers and curtains for her.

Mrs. Heath is limited in her cognitive functioning; therefore, the worker's approach has been concrete and experimental. In helping her reshape her relationship with her son, the worker has introduced some behavior modification techniques. Bobbie has a chart; for every day he works on a task quietly for one-half hour with his mother, he receives a gold star and a piece of candy. If Mrs. Heath works with her son seven days a week, she is taken out to eat once a week. With direction from the caseworker, this approach is carried out at school by Bobbie's special education teacher. Seeing other educated people using the same techniques that she is using with her son has further enhanced Mrs. Heath's self-esteem. Mrs. Heath is going to participate in a group for parents with children in the special class. She is looking forward to this experience and is eager to learn more about herself and her child.

To enable a family who is known to a protective services agency to achieve a more satisfactory life style, a caseworker must know the total family situation, as well as the needs of each of the individual members. In deciding upon a mode of treatment and in establishing the goals with the client, the worker must take into account the parents' abilities to make changes, the needs of the children, and the resources available.

17 The Process of Separation

Mildred Salins
Sinofsky, MSW

Separation experiences in childhood can affect the future growth and development of a child. Separation is a loss, a change that disrupts not only the child, but also the significant "others" to the child—usually his family members. There is a disequilibrium in the unit regardless of whether the separation is voluntary or imposed from outside. I would like to discuss some cases illustrating the dynamics of separation and, specifically, the effects of separation on the child and his family.

Separation is often seen as a last resort. When all else fails, when outside support is not enough to sustain the child in his home and he is at risk, separation occurs. From the age of six months, a child is aware of change. Ideally, separation experiences should offer a child a chance to have an awareness that a change is to occur, to have an outlet for his anxiety, and to have the opportunity to experience some positives of the move. Children of all ages—but specifically the younger child—need direct experiences; the move to take place must be acted out, so the child can see the new home and then return to his old home. Verbal explanations of a move or a separation are meaningless alone. A child learns and understands as he experiences.[1]

---

1. Krugman, D. C. Working with Separation *Child Welfare*. Vol. L, 1971.

The social workers can offer these direct experiences in preplacement visits. Ideally, these visits should include the natural parents and foster parents or the natural parents and the residential school staff member. Each caretaker visits the other environment to provide the child with the feeling of a link between the old and the new. These visits give him the feeling that the two caretakers are both interested in him, that both care.

This situation is the ideal, but how often does it or can it happen? Natural parents with weak egos and little self-esteem may find it difficult to give this much initially. The nature of the circumstances surrounding placement also plays a part. Good placement can be accomplished by two foster parents or by an agency, such as a hospital, and a foster mother. The social worker's role here is to lend support and guidance and facilitate the experience, rather than to participate.

Jay L., age four, was placed in a foster home after his father had a nervous breakdown and his mother seemed unable to cope with the home situation. Because of the voluntary nature of the placement, Jay was returned to this natural mother upon her request. This return was premature. In four months, Jay again needed placement. How could Jay cope with separation again and another adjustment in a new home? Preplacement was done and, simultaneously, I helped the new foster mother to try to empathize with Jay. How must it feel to be so small and to move so many times? Jay's new foster mother was given the name of Jay's previous foster mother. They were in the same town, so one day the new mother drove Jay to visit this previous foster mother. Jay was so pleased. The foster mothers shared ideas, did things together for Jay, such as preparing him lunch. He enjoyed this interaction and was very excited when his old foster mother called him at his new home. They both cared for him. At the same time, visiting between natural mother and Jay occurred. Despite the fact that both cried and that the separation at the end of the visit was so hard, it was a good experience. Jay needed to let his mother know he hated her to leave and that he loved her. She was letting him know she cared and that the separation hurt.

Jay's mother often spent their visits in the foster home where she became interested in the foster mother's cooking abilities. She herself was learning and receiving mothering, as well as experiencing a good role model. The foster mother's ego was boosted as she felt needed and appreciated. Jay began to feel better about himself and the placement. In this situation, I acted as an educator and facilitated actions. A social worker often needs to help others express their own feelings about separation and also help them understand or empathize with others.

In summary, preplacement visits are essential, because they allow the child to experience directly. Separation work, however, does not end here. Significant individuals to the child should get involved with the placement plans and, if possible, become part of the experience. It is an ongoing process.

Many practioners feel that part of the separation process is allowing the child to have some continuity between the two settings through keeping some of his or her toys or a favored article. Sometimes a sharing of such information as "liked foods," "feeding schedules," or "habits" helps the child make an adjustment. While this practice cannot harm the child, some practioners feel it serves no purpose. A favored food at the natural home may lose its flavor in the new home or an action or schedule may not mean the same. This reaction is based on the premise that it is not the particular food, action, or toy itself, but rather who is involved in sharing it with the child.

As the child gets older, the social worker's role increases and becomes more active. It involves recognizing feelings and dealing with the experience through actions as well as words. It includes helping the child understand his new status as a foster child, the role of the agency, and the meaning of the move to him. It means pointing up the positives of the move as well as allowing for the negatives.

Separation work, however, does not end with the child. The reverberations of the loss are felt within the family unit. Robbie B. was voluntarily placed because his mother felt she could not cope with his hyperactive, destructive behavior. She felt she hated him; at the outset, she decided he would be released for adoption at some point in the future. She did not want to see him or even talk about him—out of sight, out of mind. She denied her feelings; yet she increasingly felt miserable when I visited for our weekly sessions. I often was greeted by "Oh, I forgot it was Thursday" or "Ugh, it's Thursday already." My visit was a painful reminder of the existence of her child—one she wanted to forget.

Drew, an older sibling in the home, rarely mentioned Robbie; yet he often clung to his mother and recently was afraid to go to school. He began to become more mischievous and often questioned that, if he were bad, should he run away? Robbie had disappeared. Maybe if Drew were bad, he might too. When I was on vacation the feelings, long suppressed and repressed by the family, came to the surface. My visits did not occur. Drew began to ask his mother questions about Robbie and his own mischievous behavior began to increase. Mrs. B. became frantic, so she was pleased and anxious about our next session. My "disappearance" was upsetting to Drew. As long as I came, Robbie just might come home—or at least he was a reality.

In many following sessions Robbie was discussed with Drew. He was very interested to know if Robbie could say Drew's name; what Drew was wondering was if Robbie remembered him. He needed some reassurance that Robbie was still a person. After several questions, Drew brought me out a stuffed Snoopie dog, obviously well worn. He hugged it, then asked me if I'd take it to Robbie. Mrs. B. identified this dog as Drew's favorite toy, one with which he had never parted; yet he wanted to send it to his brother—a sort of concrete gift of his love. Mrs. B.'s eyes filled. She hugged Drew and verbally exclaimed that Robbie was loved and missed.

At this point, Mrs. B. was freed to talk more about Robbie; she began to deal with the separation and its effect on the family. Drew, age five, sat in on the discussion. He seemed relieved and was able to express his feelings about missing Robbie, as well as his concern that he would be next. His fantasies were somewhat altered. A later visit between the two brothers allowed Drew to visit Robbie in the foster home. This visit let Drew see the positives of the foster home and see that Robbie was well and happy. It was another step in the separation process. The other side of this visit was that Drew would return to his own home—a reinforcement that he was not going to leave there. Mrs. B. could not consent to her own participation at this time; yet she did see the importance of it for the two boys.

Each family member must mourn the loss, grieve, come to terms with the loss, and alter his position in the family unit. Separation is a continuous process occurring over a long period of time. Each individual's reactions and experiences are different—yet the process is similar. There is an outpouring of emotion, generally a verbal dealing with it, a desire to share the good or virtues of the individual, and then a readjustment. The process is necessary if emotional growth is to continue.

Separation as viewed by the child can mean further rejection. It can cement many negative feelings the child already has acquired. However, if the parents are involved—are part of the plan—it can be a better, even positive experience for the child and the family. The child can still feel he belongs to someone and is part of the family. For the parent or parents, their own involvement can help them alleviate the guilt feelings, and sense of failure they feel.

The following detailed example shows how separation was handled in two situations with one mother and how she reacted to each approach.

Larry, a nine-month-old severely handicapped rubella baby, was brought to a large medical center with a fractured leg. The spiral fracture gave indication that abuse might be an issue, so legal steps were taken in behalf of the child. The mother admitted that a boyfriend inflicted the injury. She came frequently to visit Larry, but generally was not dependable about keeping appointments with the hospital social worker, was relatively nonverbal, and, in general, was uncaring. Hospital personnel saw her as unable to meet Larry's needs; they made plans to place him in a foster home. The mother was called in to sign release papers, after being told what was planned. She cancelled the appointments several times. When she finally arrived, she signed release forms without a word. She was viewed as hostile, unresponsive.

Part of the hospital's view was colored by the need to clear a bed, and the staff too felt pressured. The foster home plans did not materialize; when the mother found Larry still in the hospital, she came one weekend to take him. Because of a mix-up in orders, he was released to her. This mother was not reachable by telephone, so, at this point, I became involved. Months went by with my constantly making appointments, leaving messages, and being met by no answers at mother's home. Eventually, but sporadically, I was let in, but only for a few minutes, because mother always had an appointment or other plans. She was unsure of any stranger; in many ways she was fearful of losing control of her own child.

I found the mother to be frightened and fearful of losing Larry. I empathized with her past difficult experiences at the home. I explained our concern for Larry, but focused in rather quickly on Larry's needs rather than the mother's. The mother understood little about Larry's difficulties, specifically the problems related to rubella. She was unsure about what to do with or for him. She also began to express feelings of guilt about Larry's defect as being her fault. Much of her passivity was depression—anger turned inward—anger at the hospital, at the doctors, and even at Larry.

After several interviews which gradually increased in length, the mother was able to talk about how she could use help and what alternatives she had available. Placement was discussed as an alternative. Positives were highlighted but not pushed onto the mother. She agreed to have Larry evaluated, because it would be best for him and it would finally give her some idea of what she could do for him and expect from him. I had explained as much as I could about Larry, but a real evaluation by experts would bring the facts home to her.

While waiting for this appointment, the mother began to focus on her frustrations. Money was tight, food was short. Several appointments were used to help her explore new alternatives to her problems, such as getting surplus food. As I stood in the surplus food lines with her, I began to see her as a woman with little self-esteem, wanting to be like other young women, but feeling painfully different. Surplus food generally is packed in boxes. As we approached the head of the line, the mother began her query about whether bags were available instead of boxes. Puzzled, I went along with this. On the way home, the mother exclaimed, "Welfare food comes in boxes, store-bought food comes in bags." The mother's food was in bags. After this experience, the mother begun to trust me more and feel that I was interested. I too learned from her.

Finally, when the hospital evaluation was to take place, all hospital personnel involved were alerted to the mother's needs. It was planned to give to her as much as possible, making this experience a positive one. The evaluation, sensitively done and related to the mother, pointed out that she was not at fault for Larry's disabilities; she was a good mother, but that any mother in her situation needed help. Larry was a special child. The mother was given some things she might do, but the idea that she and I had previously explored as an alternative to home care, residential placement, was brought up by the hospital staff. This evaluation occurred more than six months after I became involved with the case.

The mother was actively involved in finding places and exploring them with me. Positives were pointed up where necessary, and places were compared. Once a residential setting was found, the mother was still ambivalent. Constant support—focus on the positive of the situation and Larry's potential benefit—helped relieve her guilt. She had done well, but Larry needed special schooling help too. The mother agreed to placement and was involved with preplacement visits, but she made little effort to visit afterwards.

I suggested a visit in which we could go together. For a young girl with needs of her own, relatively isolated, and having little self-esteem, it was hard to reach out, especially to enter into a new place with new people. The mother was pleased about the visit; she requested that the maternal great-grandmother, who had raised her, join us. Great-grandmother's approval of the school pleased the mother. She could now feel surer of her decision; she was a good mother.

The mother's appearance began to improve around this time. She seemed happier and began to slowly reach out, doing things such as calling the school. Because of the great support for her actions she received at home and at the school, she was able to visit by herself and set up a schedule directly with the school personnel. The mother was noticeably less depressed. She was less isolated because she allowed herself to become involved with others in the community who had children at the same residential setting. The mother was beginning to feel better about herself, so she began to talk about herself and her problems.

In this situation, the focus initially was on Larry's medical problem rather than the mother's problem or the abuse. I listened to her view of the problem, involved her in finding alternatives, and made Larry's problem clearer to her. As well as helping her direct her efforts, these discussions also relieved her guilt about everything being her fault. A secondary gain of the evaluation was a corrective experience. This was the same hospital and many of the same personnel involved in the initial placement try. This time they better understood the mother's feelings. The focus on Larry's problem was less threatening. The mother learned to trust, to develop a relationship. The experience was positive, and it allowed her to move on to other relationships and grow.

Visiting as part of placement and separation serves the purpose of keeping ties with the family. In this example, Larry is severely handicapped; yet he too benefited as he got special mothering when his mother visited. The mother's visiting also reminded her of her family, her son, and she was learning to meet responsibilities and to cope with situations.

For a normal or older child, visiting is a direct involvement with the family. It gives him roots—a sense of belonging. He also can see the family as being good and having some positives; part of this view helps him form his self-image. "They are good, I am part of them; therefore, I am good."

Thus far, I have dealt with the feelings of the family and the identified child. What about our feelings? As social workers, professional people, we have feelings of our own that are shaped by positive and negative separation and loss experiences. We are human, caring individuals. We are advocates of the child and, in situations around abuse, we can see ourselves as "rescuers," or "saviors of the child." How can we not draw on our own past? How can we not feel? Can we be in the midst of something and not get touched? With each separation experience we are involved in as a social worker, we too must deal with ourselves. So we too experience and grow.

18 Dynamics of Separation and Placement

Ann L. Arvanian, ACSW

One of the most painful and careful decisions that we are called upon to make is that of placement of a child. Sometimes the circumstances leading to this decision give us no choice and the decision is obvious; in other cases we seem to play an omnipotent, almost God-like role. Sometimes we see ourselves as rescuing the child or children from a dangerous home situation, but is this what the child sees? He or she is not aware that we see placement as safer and as a place where his or her needs will be met. He sees his basic need as security; being with his parents represents this security.

After graduate school, my first employment was with the Division of Child Guardianship of the Department of Public Welfare. I had been working only two days when I was assigned the case of Joey, who was three. He had been placed since he was about one and one-half years old in a variety of foster homes. Deliberately physically abused by his parents, he had many healed fractures. Joey had inadvertently been emotionally abused by our society—by the succession of five or six social workers, each of whom handled his "case" and then transferred it to the next worker, losing track of the child and his parents—by the whole

117

118

legal structure that does not prevent this type of situation—by the foster parents who kept him for brief periods and then passed him on to the next set of parents. This emotional abuse was inadvertent, but it happened.

Joey was an appealing, plump, cuddly, tow-headed child. His current set of foster parents could no longer keep him, so they requested immediate placement. Joey met me that day and also had a preplacement visit with the new foster parents. They seemed mutually to like one another, so a few days later, he was placed there. Within twenty-four hours, I received a desperate phone call from these new foster parents, saying that they could not stand the child one minute more and that they had not realized they could feel this hostile toward a child. Their whole life was disrupted, and they did not want to try to work on the problem with the child in their home; they insisted on immediate removal. (They did accept a referral to another agency for counselling for themselves.)

I located a new foster home that would take Joey and picked him up in my car—a sobbing, terrified child. He felt he had been "bad" and the punishment was removal. This reaction often happens with children who are removed from their own home. They feel that they have first been abused because they were "bad" and then abandoned by their parents as a further punishment. Over and over Joey cried, "I want to go home, I want to go home!" But there was no home. There was a place where I would take him with a house and parents, but no home.

When the decision was made to place this child, rather than work with the parents to keep him with them, how could it have been predicted that this child's life would be so painful and unstable? Is he ever going to feel a sense of "home" anywhere in the world at any age?

In making the decision to place any child, there are so very many factors to consider—and there are good ways to handle placement. We strive toward the best possible handling, or really the ideal, while battling the reality of situations that turn out like Joey's did.

One factor to consider in making the placement decision is what the end result will be for a number of parties: the family unit and the extended family, the foster parents, and the child. Consider just a few things that could happen to these parties.

Within the family, when one member is removed, roles shift. This shifting is particularly important when the child removed has been a scapegoat and the family juggles its positions to give this role to another child. Other times, the entire family structure disintegrates. Often the parents are made to feel much guilt by their own parents; even the relationship between generations breaks asunder.

The foster family is a complete family in itself. Consider the ideal foster family—warm, affectionate, yet capable of setting limits with children. Then, add a new factor—a child who has learned how to provoke adults. Take the example of Joey. Early in life he learned that he received attention from his parents by provoking abuse. He seeks to recapture his lost parent by attempting very hard to provoke the same familiar behavior that represents mother or father and "home" to him. The foster parents cannot allow themselves to respond in this manner; they have to teach the child a new way of seeking attention.

One very important factor is how the foster parents view the child's real parents. The child forms his self-image in part from his view of his parents. It is hard for the foster parents not to compete with the child's real parents, and not to point out how many good things they do for the child—as opposed to how badly the child was treated by his own parents. They have to allow and encourage the child's positive as well as angry and sad feelings toward the real parents. All of this is a herculean task for the best of foster parents.

The end result for the child can sometimes be tragic. Look for a moment at the adult who develops from the child who has grown up in a foster home. It is not just chance that many of the clients served by social service agencies have grown up apart from their parents. A great many of the mothers and fathers I've spoken with have said, "I don't know how to be a parent. I just don't know how. I've never had one." One other thing I've noticed in adults who as children were separated from their parents is a longing to find and know their own parents. They feel that, if they can just know their parents, they will find a part of themselves. Their whole sense of identity has been impaired by the separation. It is pertinent to note that the basis of psychoanalytic theory revolves around the bond between children and parents; impaired adult functioning can be traced back to malfunctions within the child-parent relationship, with separation being one of the most crucial situations.

Looking at the child who has been separated, we see a grieving child—grieving not only for his lost parents, but for the whole familiar environment and family structure that is all he has known; grieving for a part of himself. Loss is so painful for any of us, even as adults. Loss by death is perhaps the most grievous, but even a change in location or jobs can precipitate a sense of loss. Imagine the child, whose whole image of the world is based upon his parents and environment, having to lose these. He does not perceive that he is safer away from this situation, not neglected or abused in this new home. He knows only that he has lost a part of himself. The emotions triggered in a child are sadness, grief, and an overwhelming sense of detachment. He feels abandoned. He shows regression and also angry behavior. All of these things might remain with him to a pathological degree throughout most of his life. There is a duality of the scar tissue he carries—some from the pain of abuse and neglect and some from a sense of loss—some external scars perhaps, and many internal ones.

Another factor influencing our decision is the length of foreseeable placement. Duration of placement falls within one of three categories:

1. *A short-term placement during a family crisis.* In this instance, there is a high return potential. I have used this type of placement a number of times. In one case during a mother's hospitalization for psychosis, when the father also became overwhelmed and depressed over the mother's hospitalization, a preschool child was placed for about a month. He was then reunited, and he has been with his parents for the past two years. Just recently, he has become very sad and has been clinging to his parents. The reaction seems to correlate with the season; this is the time of year when he was placed. So, even in this type of situation, the child shows many emotional scars.

2. *Long-term and permanent placement—when, generally, parents have very little interest in the child being placed.* These cases are obvious almost from the beginning. An example is an adolescent girl who grew up in an abusive home situation with alcoholic parents. This case finally reached court with custody permanently removed from the parents. She was placed with a neighbor, where she has remained for the past few years. During these years, she has been a member in an adolescent group with which I am working. Her own family disintegrated, but her position in the foster family is secure. However, she becomes depressed and fearful whenever there is any illness in the foster family.
   One of the problems in the placement, even though successful, is that the foster mother has competed with the child's real mother, so the child has a hard time expressing her love and longing for her real mother. She does use the group as an outlet for her positive feelings because they are accepted here. When we had an angel cake at one of our meetings, her face lighted up and she said, "My mother used to make cakes like this," as she ate the whole thing. So, even though the placement is long-term or permanent, this child still needs to share her positive feelings about her real parents as well as her anger at them. The foster parents can accept her anger towards her parents, but not her love for them. She needs to deal with all of her feelings towards her parents.

3. *Indefinite, unknown placement.* This third type of placement, perhaps the most difficult to interpret to the child and the most difficult to work with, deals with the child in limbo. Will the child be reunited with his own parents, in foster care indefinitely, or with adoptive parents?

Joey is an example of the third type of placement. Another situation of this type involved a family in which the divorced mother was not in a position to care for her children. I was forced to go to court to remove her two preschool children from her custody. She later requested of the court that the children be permanently placed, but not adopted, as she was not sure how long it would take to get herself together so that she could give them proper care. For two and one-half years, they have been placed—together. The mother visits them nearly every week. She still is unsure when she will be able to resume full-time care of them. The children are showing some problems, but they have not suffered from the total loss of their parent or from the loss of each other. So, the trauma of separation has, at least, been as minimal as possible.

It is most important that all children, whether placed in foster homes, residential treatment centers, or group homes, receive continuity of care and continuity of some parenting persons. In one family, the children were placed and then returned to an improved yet precarious home situation. In this family, I represent security to the children. The problem with the social worker representing the family stability to the children is that professionals do shift jobs fairly frequently, and the children must again experience loss of what they felt was a stable person in their lives.

I will not dwell on what types of placements are best for what types of children, since it is an enormous subject. Usually, the ideal placement is not available, so we work with what we have. There are many good foster homes, group homes, residential treatment centers—but, as we all know, not enough. We all want each child that must be placed to have the best possible placement—but sometimes this is not available.

Often the decision to place a child is not ours to make. Sometimes circumstances lead us to an "easy" decision. Often court action helps us decide. Whether placement is voluntary or involuntary, all of the same issues play a part. A word of caution though—when a parent requests placement, we should explore carefully before agreeing with this decision. Perhaps it is not the right decision for them and we can work with them so that they will want to keep the child. The same reasoning holds true for foster parents who occasionally give up the care of a foster child who presents enormous problems.

How do we help a family work through placement? With whom do we work—the parents? the foster parents? the child? Ideally, we work with all three.

One couple I worked with placed an adolescent son reluctantly and gave him double messages; he would leave his foster placement and run back to his parents. When his parents and I talked about it, I likened it to King Solomon, who, when each of two women claimed an infant was hers, offered to cut the child in half. One woman refused, saying that the other could have the whole child, rather than have the child cut in half. King Solomon recognized that this was the real mother, who would rather give up the child than have him destroyed. It is so important to help the parents feel good about the decision to place, when this seems to be the appropriate decision. The foster parents also need to feel good about what they are doing; they need much interpretation about what is happening and how best to adjust to this child who is now a member in their family. The child needs to be able to express his or her feelings of grief, of anger, and of love for his own parents.

How long should treatment continue? There is really no set time. Treatment and acceptance of the placement has to be an ongoing process. As in treatment of any patient or client, we treat them until they have worked it through or have themselves gained an ability to keep on working it through.

Placement and separation are such drastic steps to take. All of the foregoing discussion merely touches on some of the things involved. I firmly believe that we should all try—as I think we do—to work with the intact family toward overcoming the problems of neglect and abuse. People are so remarkably adaptive. Children can adapt to a tragic home-life and, with help, even to separation. So, too, with help, can abusing and neglecting parents adapt themselves to a different pattern of interaction with children than they have had. Still, sometimes placement is necessary, for the safety of the child; in those cases, the decision making should be as careful and thorough as possible—weighing separation and placement as a viable yet potentially disastrous alternative. We must ensure that the added suffering we are having to impose on the child is as much lessened as possible.

Perhaps together we can share with each other new ways of handling this painful problem—perhaps, in the future, eliminating situations like Joey's.

19 The Social Worker's Use of the Court

Shirl E. Fay, ACSW

Inevitably, a social worker or anyone with responsibilities to families and the protection of children working in this area for any period of time must anticipate use of the court in dealing with serious situations of neglect or abuse. Although this occurrence is not frequent a social worker must be able, willing, and committed to move a family situation into the neutral setting of a courtroom and to seek the help of lawyers and the decisions of a judge in an attempt to help a family. A juvenile judge has the right—and the responsibility—to protect children. He or she can act on their behalf, can issue orders to help families, and, as a catalyst, can often force drastic action and implement changes.

Making use of a court is a critical decision; court action should not be initiated until all other attempts to help a family have been exhausted. Those of us involved in the area of child welfare know well the trauma of separation and the risks of placement. When this course of action is necessary, however, we cannot back away from the responsibility of using the courts—viewing this action as a tool in treatment and hoping this avenue will be therapeutic for the family.

Making a decision to use the courts to help a family is an extremely

123

serious one. It demands a careful evaluation of the total family situation and a diagnostic assessment of the family members (including their ability to make changes). It also requires an honest appraisal of whether or not the social worker has indeed tried all possible ways to help and all methods of treatment toward the improvement of a deteriorated situation.

In some situations, there is time to move at a slow and steady pace. In others, it is apparent upon initial contact that the circumstances of a child, physically or emotionally, are so acutely inadequate that court action must be used immediately. This action should be used whenever children are in real danger; we should be able to recognize and assess these situations and act promptly when it is necessary. We should also be ready to act quickly in the courts when it is clear after a few contacts that too much time would be needed to effect change by other methods; court action is needed to avoid irreversible damage to children.

Moving into court must be seen as a helpful, positive tool; such action is not being pursued because the social worker is frustrated, angry, and therefore feeling punitive toward the family. Sorting out our feelings and being aware of our attitudes are vital when we work with any family situation. These processes are absolutely necessary in an objective decision to request the court's authority to provide a better situation for the family and to provide protection for children.

Hopefully, if various people or agencies have been working together to help a family, such an important decision could be a mutual one of the concerned people. All the participants would willingly agree to help directly during the court appearance, especially appearing as witnesses when necessary. Unfortunately, knowledgeable individuals with vital material pertaining to the protection of children often are unwilling to, or are restricted by agency policy from, sharing knowledge with the court unless a subpoena has been issued. The strength needed in court situations and the help to families are diminished when these restrictions are imposed. Anger is stirred up on all sides when people feel it is an imposition to have to be a witness in a stressful court situation.

Sometimes an agency concerned about its community image fears that going to court will mean being looked at as an agency which "takes away children." The agency fears that its relationships with other people in the community will be destroyed. Actually, neighbors or friends of a family, as well as other professionals, often feel court action has not been taken soon enough. Primarily, though, if we are committed to helping families and children, we must be willing to share all useful information with a judge so that the decision can be a sound and fair one.

The social worker using the court system must be secure and clear in his or her thinking and evaluation of the family. There can be no ambivalence or uncertainty that this is the best plan for the family. It is sometimes very difficult after working for improvements with a family for some time to reach the conclusion—and share our concern with the family—that the situation has not improved enough; despite our joint efforts, we are going to ask the court for help. Help in this instance is approaching the court and asking a judge to assist a family by making a critical decision that may mean children will be separated from their parents.

The family, which may have had difficulty trusting us throughout our contact, may feel betrayed, deceived, and angry—although they are often relieved that a decision has been made for them. Many parents' feelings of being inadequate, unworthy, and rejected become sharpened. Although the parents may not hear—or understand—immediately, it must be emphasized to them that it is only because we care, because we need to protect their children, and because we want the best for the family, that going to court is necessary.

It is not uncommon to give a family one more opportunity if there is any agreement at all that there can be improvements. However, it is unfair to parents and to children to perpetuate an inadequate or dangerous situation. Social workers often say—after finally deciding to use the court and going through the proceedings—that they wished they had initiated court action sooner. This reaction follows situations where, because of a judge's order, a family makes drastic changes not previously made. The reaction also follows a judge's decision to place children in foster homes when parents cannot cope with their overwhelming life situations and are relieved by the removal of the responsibility they can not handle. There are, however, some disappointing and shattering experiences when a judge may return children to what the social worker sees as a disorganized, inadequate, or dangerous family situation where there seems to be no hope for improvement.

Many different situations come to the attention of agencies, hospitals, nursing services, or others who are working in the area of child abuse and neglect. We see infants bruised or physically injured; children who are not fed or clothed, who do not go to school; children of a parent who is alcohol or drug addicted; children caught in the midst of constant arguments and fights between adults where a parent may be physically injured or hurt; children who are regularly unsupervised or are in dangerous situations. We also see the child who is clothed, fed, and sent to school, but is unloved and rejected, is ignored, or is not allowed to play with friends. There is the child who is constantly yelled at or put down by his parent, or who must constantly supervise his younger siblings or care for an emotionally starved parent. These children are just as much at risk emotionally as those who are physically deprived.

When is it, however, that we turn to the court for help? Some of the instances might be when we have not been able to help an abusive parent to control his or her impulses, so the angry and dangerous outbursts continue; or when depressed, neglecting parents continue, in spite of our efforts, to be unable to give their children proper physical care; or when an alcohol- or drug-addicted parent cannot seek necessary help for a debilitating problem directly interfering with the care of children; or when marital problems cannot be resolved, so a mother and father continue their alarming physical battles.

It is important that we also turn to the court when parents cannot improve the emotional climate for a child: when, for instance, a mother or father prohibits normal development or socialization of a child; or when a parent cannot adjust to or try to change his or her severely rejecting attitudes toward a child, and continues the scapegoating process. We should use the court whenever we need to guarantee the protection of a child. As social workers in protective services, we have an obligation to help parents improve the care of their children using every means available to us. We have the further obligation to use the court to help us, if necessary, when we have put forth our best efforts and the parents have not been able to respond to them.

Involving the court is a decision reached as part of the treatment process. It is a vital component of the continuum of service we offer: reaching out to a troubled family and sharing our concern; offering services and treatment; utilizing community resources—other helping people or concrete services, such as day care or homemaker to help alleviate pressures and share some of the overwhelming child care responsibilities; supporting the parents and their efforts; carefully and earnestly evaluating and assessing the home situation with all involved; moving into court to help a family if it becomes clear that parents need this additional, therapeutic help without which their children would be deprived of basic rights.

Do we always achieve what we hope through a hearing in a courtroom? Is this sometimes tedious and difficult process valuable? Is the time consumed the best use of our time? Are courts receptive to our efforts and requests? Will a judge's decision really help the family concerned? The answers do vary. As well as being persons in positions of power, judges are people, with their own personalities and bases of knowledge. Some have more experience in child development; they know the physical and emotional needs of children and, in turn, know what happens to children who do not receive proper stimulation and good care. Some may tend to be subjective, using their own life experiences to determine what a child needs. Many judges simply feel a child belongs with his parents; they cannot make any decision that would mean separation. However, many other judges carefully consider all of the information available to them and make hard decisions after honest appraisals of all facts presented. This consideration, after all, is what we have requested, even if sometimes the decision does not agree with our recommendation.

Parents and children should have the opportunity to be represented by separate counsel who can consider the total family situation as well as their individual clients. For instance, it is not helpful for a lawyer to be such an advocate for an abusive parent that a judge is persuaded to send a child home, where no changes have been made and where the pathology will continue to the detriment of the child. It is advantageous for the family if the social workers and lawyers can work together, share their goals with one another, and come in a purposeful manner to a mutual understanding about the family's needs.

When we work with troubled families, we make an investment to try to help. Our continuous concern must be guaranteed. When we cannot bring about sufficient change to provide a better environment for children—with our treatment methods alone or with support from the community—we must use the courts. Not using this resource, when appropriate, can deprive a child of protection and a family of possible help and structure which might benefit them. While court experience can be involved and complicated, it can also offer the satisfaction that we have utilized every community resource available to protect children. Hopefully, this course of action will be therapeutic; it will be a positive and useful tool as we work to improve life for families in trouble.

PART SIX

COMMUNITY
RESOURCES

20 The Use of Community Resources in Work with Abusive Families

Joanne D. Lipner,
ACSW

The use of community resources in the handling of the problem of child abuse depends upon an early diagnostic evaluation. An early dispositional conference will often clarify what stresses the family is functioning under, who needs to be involved with the family, and how help can best be offered.

Once it is established that a child can be safe in his own home if a system of supports is built in, it is necessary also to determine what kind of service is most appropriate for the individual needs of a given family. Perhaps an overview of the nature of community services will give us some insight into how agencies might better use and develop these resources for the benefit of abusing parents and their children.

It has been our increasing experience in the helping professions that we do not necessarily need a bachelor's degree and/or a master's degree in social work to provide effective service to families in need of outside intervention. The consistent and supportive involvement of a good friend is often the very key to a change in the parent-child relationship in families where child abuse has occurred. Very often this service can best be offered by the paraprofessional employee or volunteer. Mature adults

131

willing to take on these most troubled families exist in nearly every community. It is important to note here that compassion and the desire to help—although admirable qualities—are not enough. The parent-aide must be able to focus on the needs of parents and not the children—trusting that, if parents improve, so will the children—thus arises the term parent-aide. Empathy, gentleness, patience, and the basic capacity to mother and love are important to the success of the paraprofessional's work with abusing parents. Very often, having lived through the difficult experiences which come with marriage and parenting is an invaluable asset. The role of the parent-aide varies with individual families. At times, the primary role is to sit over a cup of coffee with a mother so isolated from her own extended family and community that this very human sharing is an unknown experience. Much of the parent-aides' work involves helping parents to use other community resources which they themselves may have taken advantage of at one time. Other services are helping with clinic appointments and with shopping. It all adds up to addressing ourselves to the reality that all battering parents were battered themselves emotionally and/or physically and to building into their lives nurturing experiences that will enable them to meet their children's needs.

I am not suggesting that the paraprofessional's involvement with the family be necessarily the only "rescue" provided. It has been our experience that a caseworker's involvement is essential—although the relationship may be more intense with either helping person. A team approach to the handling of families in crisis has multiple benefits in terms of beginning the re-parenting process. Although there may be some overlap, the importance of a family's coming to know that more than one person cares can far outweigh the overlap. If a good collaboration exists between the caseworker and the parent-aide, both will be aware of their individual—and equally valuable—roles with the family in working toward a common goal. In addition to the benefits for the family, we have discovered that shared responsibility for services relieves much of the stress and strain in working with abusive parents. All who offer help to families in crisis need supervision and a forum to air feelings connected with this work in order to promote effectiveness with the family.

Another use of the paraprofessional employee or volunteer is in direct service to children. This use can only be effected if the child is in foster care or in a day care program. If the child is in his own home, all attention must be focused on the parents because their overwhelming needs interfere with their ability to see children as having needs of their own.

In March, 1974, the Welfare Department in partnership with the Junior League of Boston opened an infant day care center on James

Street in the South End of Boston. The center serves 12 children at risk in their own homes; in addition to full-time professional child care personnel, it is staffed by volunteers from the Junior League. The understanding and affection these very upset children have received from the volunteers cannot be measured.

One of the most difficult tasks for the volunteer is to realize that these children, who appear socially precocious and advanced for their age, have never had an opportunity to be babies. In many instances this situation defines the primary role of the volunteer: to allow the children the freedom to be children—to express their feelings, whatever they may be, and to accept them as individuals. The volunteer's ability to meet the child's negative and positive feelings enables him or her to rest upon the strength of an adult who has accepted both strength and weakness as part of man.

The children attending the day care center are transported daily to and from their homes. Here again, the driver plays an important role in the nurturing process for both parents and children. Essential is an ability to demonstrate patience and gentleness with mothers who have difficulty having the children ready on time in the morning and who sometimes forget that someone must be at home to receive the child in the afternoon.

The parents respond by gradually being able to meet the expectations of time limits. Perhaps this point seems minor, but it can be a milestone for parents who have never known the smallest sense of accomplishment. The driver's relationship with the children is vital as well. The morning pick-up time is often stressful; it must be met by the driver with calm and with understanding of the child's need for reassurance. Once more the child has an opportunity to experience relationship with a mature adult ready and willing to meet his needs.

Homemaker services for abusive parents can be an essential part of the treatment process. Success, however, with this use of a community resource, depends on careful planning and an awareness of the qualities necessary for effective service. The homemaker must be neither a therapist nor a spy for the agency. Most of our clients have experienced poverty, desertion by important people in their lives, discrimination, and pushing around. The homemaker must be sensitive to these realities. Overefficiency and briskness on the part of the homemaker will make the parents feel more helpless and inadequate. Homemaker service for families in which child abuse has occurred calls for an individual who can provide an experience in mothering for parents in addition to providing help and relief in terms of home management. Although the homemaker is not expected to deal with or to treat the problems as she encounters them, she must be alert to them and must know how to recognize them and refer them properly and speedily. It does not take a skilled professional therapist to deal with the problem of "insufficient mothering." The supportive person who works along with parents in a gentle way when household relief is necessary can be essential to the preservation of the family as a unit and to the prevention of child abuse.

The visiting nurse is yet another community resource that can be utilized to benefit abusive parents. I stress here—once more—that an understanding of the dynamics of child abuse is essential for therapeutic entry into the family. The primary job of a visiting nurse is not to check on parents, supervise them, or give very much advice. A sympathetic listener who does not obviously teach provides another experience in mothering for abusive parents. When suspicion of and anger toward institutions and authority is overtly expressed by parents, it is often only the visiting nurse who can connect directly with the family. At times, a medical person can be accepted by battering parents much more readily, particularly at the beginning of our work with a family.

One community resource seldom given full recognition as one of the mainstays in child welfare is foster care. When separation of parents from the child is the only treatment alternative, it is, of course, necessary to plan carefully how the child will be cared for outside his own home. Extended family relationships are usually pathological; placement of a child with relatives can reinforce unhealthy interaction among family members and between parent and child.

The experience of a good foster home placement can be beneficial for both abusive parents and their children. If foster parents have an ability to examine their feelings of anger at the abuse and take responsibility for these feelings, they can be an essential key in a therapeutic approach to the problem. The job requires a twenty-four hour kind of commitment to a child who most often cannot return their caring. By its very nature, foster care implies a temporary arrangement. It is a process in which effective foster parents not only provide security and protection, but also a bridge between the natural home and the child. We are all aware of the importance of biological ties. This bridge can be provided between the child and his heritage even if his own parents are not a physical reality for him. Of course, all involved—natural parents, foster parents, and the child—must have a continuing opportunity to air feelings around the issues of placement and future planning.

The result of the kind of life experience of abusive parents and their children is that the primary concern is survival. Today is what counts with them. Lifelines must be provided.

We are convinced that within the wealth of experience in the field of family services there are numbers of resources to help us make more sense to segments of the community most caught up in crisis. However, to make use of this experience appropriately, it is necessary to depart from established methodology. We must use freely our knowledge and skills to develop methods of using resources in the community that can relate specifically to the group we are choosing to help. We must be prepared for a long period of testing as to our sincerity. We have found that it is possible to be effective in changing long-established patterns of violence in the family through the appropriate use of community resources.

21 The Use of Specialized Day Care in Preventing Child Abuse

Shirley L. Bean, ACSW

Four years ago, Parents' and Children's Services established a program for the study and prevention of child abuse. While the program provides simultaneous treatment for both parents and children, this chapter will emphasize the day care aspect of the program rather than the work with parents, which is also an integral part of our approach.

Our project, called the Parents' Center, grew out of the combined awareness of the agency's staff and its consultant psychiatrist of the need to offer innovative preventive services to a growing number of families where abuse of children was suspected or a pattern of abuse was developing. These families' problems included situations of harsh and unusual punishment, deliberate deprivation of food, physical or medical care, or excessive verbal expression of anger.

We conceived of the Center as a setting for both parents and children. To be considered were those families in which the parents had serious personality defects which were reflected in inappropriate behavior toward their children. In such families, the children's needs could not be fully met in their own homes; yet the children would be harmed rather than helped by full-time placement. We planned this setting to be one where the activity and experience of both parents and children could be utilized for treatment purposes. Our purpose was to demonstrate ways to help parents who are having difficulty controlling their behavior toward their children.

The primary treatment approach would be group treatment led by a male and a female therapist. Individual counseling would be provided when emergencies or crises arose that were best handled outside the group. Otherwise, primary responsibility would rest with the cotherapists. We would provide supervised daytime care of the abused child during the day for at least a three-month period. Our agency's medical director would supervise any necessary medical care for these children, whose ages would range from three months through three years. Our criteria for selection of families included an incident of abuse or suspected abuse, one-parent families or two-parent families with both parents living in the home, and parents amenable to help and willing to attend the group meetings. These families also needed to be living geographically near enough to the Center to facilitate transportation.

We then involved the community by holding a series of meetings with representatives of key community agencies most likely to come in contact with the families we wanted to identify. Of greatest importance was the task of finding child care workers who could be helped to respond to the testing-out on the part of parents without defensiveness and without anger. We experimented with a variety of aides and assistants. Housewives, college students, and board members joined our program to act as drivers, child care workers, cooks, and sometimes social workers, too. The agency homemaker service was drawn into the program at points of crisis. We soon learned the importance of maintaining lines of staff communication by means of regular meetings, as well as the necessity for coordinating work among agencies already involved with the families.

All in all, there were times when we thought we had taken on more than we could handle. At these times, we relied heavily on our own weekly psychiatric consultation meetings for support. Our teamwork approach has enabled us to bear the anxiety which otherwise would be unendurable. We share and compare observations and explore their significance with other members of the team. This approach affords relief and balances the burden of anxiety.

One of our first findings in pursuing appropriate cases was that many workers were reluctant to refer parents to the center because the referral required explicit discussion of the worker's concern about the possibility of abuse. Many times the referring workers' own conflicted feelings prevented them from bringing this possibility out in the open. From the beginning, our position has been that it would afford the parents emotional relief to be able to discuss their tendencies toward abusiveness with a worker who expressed willingness to understand and who asserted confidence in his ability to help.

Ours has been a small demonstration project. To date, 36 families have been involved in the Parents' Center with 59 children between the ages of three months and four years. The results of our treatment approach with both parents and children have been most gratifying. We intervene when parents feel unable to cope. We build in ways to assist them to handle themselves differently and to deal more effectively with their situation. The results have confirmed our premise that parents can change if given the opportunity with certain environmental and emotional resources made available. The sharing of responsibility for the child through the use of our Center frees the parents of the pressures long enough to sit back and, with our professional help, look at what has happened in their lives.

At the weekly group meetings, parents of children at the Center discuss their experiences and concerns about themselves, their marriages, and their children, with the goal of separating their own difficulties from those attributable to their child. Initially, many parents fear removal of the child from them. It is as though they expect to be punished for an emotional illness. After these initial feelings come expressions of loneliness and isolation. With such impoverishment in their relationships, it is no wonder the child becomes such an important object in their lives—both as a loved and a hated one.

Parents come to the group with all kinds of assumptions—but mainly that everyone is better than they are. They begin to challenge each other in the group, and this process helps correct their misperceptions about themselves. The group offers an opportunity to fill the gaps in their social and emotional relationships with other people. They begin to see their uniqueness, and they can improve their reality-testing. As they begin to come to grips with their own problems, they also begin to view their children differently. This is a *very slow* process.

In the meantime, valuable time is passing for the child. During this period we have a large role to play in contributing to the child's growth and development. The day care program provides immediate relief from what has become an oppressive situation between the parents and child. It temporarily removes the child who is the target of hostility and permits him to experience a more healthy quality of parenting. For some children who are at more risk than others, the Center gives day-to-day contact that provides both the child and the parents with a feeling of security through constancy and availability of our staff. The uniqueness of our program is that we reach children early—we accept them as young as three months of age; we give them the nurturance that they are not able to get at home. At this stage, the children cannot depend on their parents, whose behavior may be quite irrational; the children may well react by exhibiting withdrawn-passive behavior. We teach them trust and the beginnings of identification, since our staff includes male and female volunteers as well as male and female child care workers.

The Center attempts to create an environment which makes it more easy to correct or alleviate problems in the children's development and social functioning by exposing them to a different quality of interaction. A gentle and supportive—and sometimes necessarily firm—staff can help children become capable of meeting expectations, dealing adequately with daily life situations, developing a sense of self, and accepting the reality of the limitations set down by parents and others. This help requires the setting of consistent standards of behavior—not always an easy task with children whose interaction with their parents has been particularly inconsistent and unbalanced. We attempt to set limits in a nonpunitive fashion; the children's understanding of these limits helps them control themselves and become more manageable and less provocative in their behavior. Children who are relatively in control of themselves are better able to understand their capabilities and be proud of them with the support of adults. The trust fostered through this consistent adult support, coupled with emerging inner resources, broadens the child's capacity for self-expression and for relationships with other children.

As with parents, the therapeutic treatment is a gradual process—although the children respond much more quickly and thoroughly than their parents. We have found that the most effective way to accomplish our goals, depending on the individual child, is consistent and warm structuring on the part of the child care workers. This consistency arises from daily routines which structure the activities of daily living so that children know what to expect and when to expect it, as well as knowing what is expected of them. Daily routines give the children the security of the familiar and the strength of continuity. The children generally progress to the point where they can coordinate their motor capacities to aid in the fulfillment of their needs, and they come to display initiative, imagination, and the capacity to play. The children become able to call for adult attention and express their needs through words and gestures instead of by violent and uncontrolled aggression.

I would now like to describe briefly the development and experiences of one of our youngsters, Danny, age three, who arrived at the Center a very quiet, contained, and unhappy little boy. While he appeared small for his age, he was well fed and in good health. He and his two siblings, one older and one younger, experienced several foster home placement separation periods from their family during particularly stressful situations. Danny had just returned home for the third time only a few days before he entered the program. He reacted to all of this turmoil and confusion with apathetic and passive behavior. The complex family problems, coupled with Danny's background of separation experiences, contributed to a fairly incomprehensible world for so young a child. An all-pervasive insecurity and an unawareness of what was expected of him created a very passive and listless child. The terror of his inconsistent world had made him cautious and fearful of angering others; he shrank from exposing himself to notice and played it safe by doing very little. He did not communicate with or interact with any of the other children. Most of Danny's time was spent on the periphery of activities, listlessly sitting or lying around looking miserable. He had an excessive control of his feelings and a limited range of facial expressions. His physical movements appeared to be quite self-contained and constricted.

After a few days at the Center, Danny's behavior demonstrated an almost frantic quality of need to manipulate the adult staff, the only people with whom he would interact. Danny was desperately trying to structure and control the situation by demanding that the staff do certain activities the way he wanted them done—for example, "You sit there" or "Pick me up." There was a ritualistic quality to his attempts to communicate; he would dwell on such facts as the colors of his clothes and such procedures as "When I get up from my nap, John will come and take me home to mommy." This fairly rigid, insecure, dependent behavior continued for at least a month and a half. His inability to express his needs was almost complete; in most cases, he didn't even attempt it. Not one other child at the Center would have sat quietly and miserably while another child stole his piece of cake.

Gradually Danny began to play on a very limited basis with one particular child, even though his most comfortable moments remained those spent in a one-to-one relationship with an adult. After Danny had been at the Center more than two months, we observed a definite change and improvement in his behavior and self-assertion. He became very daring and provocative; with or without provocation, he would kick, hit, and throw blocks and toys at the other children. He became more and more resistant to suggestions and requests from the staff, even though such acting-out behavior was not dealt with harshly.

Danny's behavior fluctuated between this emerging pattern and his previous methods of avoiding situations and contacts. He was able to express spontaneous joy and laughter on his trips to the park with other children; eventually, he asked to be in the back of the car with other children. He began to enjoy physical activities such as dancing the "hokey pokey" and playing games. He did much better on individual skill tasks as well. With much encouragement, he began to string beads by himself and—although he would occasionally lapse into an "I can't" —he would do so and be quite proud, along with the staff, of his accomplishments.

In the case of Danny, and all the other children, the parents who contributed to the problem of child abuse were not so quickly affected by participation in the program. Danny's parents, through their regular attendance at the weekly group meetings, are slowly learning about their difficulties in understanding and expressing their needs and how this affects their marriage and children.

Parents like Danny's are encouraged to participate at the Center in a variety of activities. One mother who had particular difficulties in separating from her youngster participated by supervising a group of children as they were being transported to the Center. Some mothers prepare and serve food, help child care workers in leading activities, or offer special talents in music, arts, and crafts. Other mothers are encouraged to come simply to observe their children in interaction with other children to help modify their high expectations of their offspring.

If we are to intervene effectively and assist families where child abuse is a primary problem, we must have a commitment from community agencies to serve these families and a variety of services and resources that can be utilized by these agencies. The need to experiment with different approaches is evident. The Parents' Center Project represents one such approach—a combination of day care for the children and counseling for the parents.

22 The Gilday Center: A Method of Intervention for Child Abuse

Leslie Gardner, MEd

In the fall of 1971, the Junior League of Boston was asked to set up a center to provide child care for certain "children at risk." This request came jointly from Parents' and Children's Services and the Inflicted Injury Unit of the Division of Family and Children's Services of the Department of Public Welfare. The project, modelled after the Parents' Center, was designed to serve children referred to the Inflicted Injury Unit. The center was designed not only to provide a healthy environment in which children could develop trust in adults and peers, but also to provide enough relief to parents so that they might better use available social services and increase their own self-esteem. It would provide social workers with a viable alternative to foster care for a child in need of protection.

In November of 1971, the League voted to organize and fund the program and to staff it for 12 to 18 months; after that time, the Inflicted Injury Unit agreed to assume operation. After several months of incredible hassles over licensing, renovations, and building inspections, the center opened for its first children on March 6, 1972. It is housed in a very old, inner-city building which was formerly a parochial high school.

Three offices were transformed with much ingenuity into space for 12 children, up to three years of age; the quarters even include a complete kitchen. A remarkable number of diverse organizations and individuals worked with the League to initiate the project. They include: the Department of Health and Hospitals; City of Boston Day Care Licensing Unit; the Inflicted Injury Unit of the Division of Family and Children's Services; the Assistant Commissioner for Social Services, Department of Public Welfare; the Parents' and Children's Services; the South End Community Health Center; the Rector of the Immaculate Conception Church (our landlord); three private physicians; and a building contractor who gave valuable practical assistance. This combination of public and private agencies, including professional and volunteer services as well as private and public funding, was unique. The Gilday Center has already served as a model for a similar project begun in September of 1973 by the Junior League of Springfield, Massachusetts.

The day care center was designed to serve children at time of family crisis. Therefore, each child's stay should extend from three to six months. Unfortunately, this optimum is not always possible, because day care resources for children under two and a half are severely limited. Flexibility is the key both in accepting with minimal delay children from the Inflicted Injury Unit's caseload and in keeping the child in the center until optimal disposition of the case can be made. After the child is accepted into the program by the intake committee and is seen at the South End Community Health Center by our consulting pediatrician, the social worker arranges a visit to the center for parent and child. Often the child begins regular attendance the next day.

In addition to the initial medical examination, the Health Center also provides ongoing medical care for any family which desires it. The center has resources available for psychiatric, vision, dental, and hearing problems and for any necessary lab work. Generally a child receives all appropriate immunizations during his stay at the center. Tests are given routinely for lead poisoning and sickle cell anemia. Our pediatrician meets with the day-care staff weekly to discuss each child's medical-social progress. He also consults on general health problems such as sanitation, head lice, nutrition, and communicable diseases. The Health Center finances these services through Medicaid.

The staff at the Gilday Center consists of the director, who has a master's degree in education and experience at Parents' Center, and two full-time child care workers, one of whom is a licensed practical nurse. The other worker has an associate's degree in child study, and she was trained as a maternal and infant care worker in the Intervention Program for High Risk Families directed by Dr. Eleanor Pavenstedt under the auspices of the Tufts-Columbia Point Health Center. In September, we added a part-time child care worker who speaks Spanish and who is receiving on-the-job training.

The most important function of the day care staff is to create an atmosphere and environment in which a child can relax and be free from tension. What becomes important is not a worker's educational background, but the warmth, humor, and openmindedness with which she relates to people. One needs to be prepared to cuddle, reprimand, teach, bathe, toilet train, diaper, feed, cook for, play with, and, generally, mother emotionally deprived children. This role takes an enormous amount of energy and inner strength. Feelings about staff and children have to be open so they can be faced and dealt with. What is ultimately created is the mutual interdependency of a family. In a setting like this, it is important to keep staff small in number and to allow time and resources for relaxing and talking honestly. The staff must relate to one another personally as well as professionally. In this kind of work, staff turnover must be minimal to achieve maximum consistency for the children. Therefore, the staff should be well paid, liberally provided with benefits, and encouraged to take advantage of educational opportunities and resources.

The Inflicted Injury Unit provides us with a coordinating social worker who is responsible for ongoing communication between social work and day care staff. Weekly meetings are held by day care staff to exchange information regarding child and family progress with individual social workers. These meetings are invaluable, since it is here that issues and feelings concerning a child can be shared and alternative methods of handling behavior are discussed.

We have recently arranged for regular consultation with the Boston University Department of Child Psychiatry. This relationship will hopefully open resources for necessary psychological evaluations. It will also provide a source of support for the day care staff. Obviously, working on a day-to-day basis with these children can be both physically and emotionally draining.

The Gilday Center has been financed through a contract of service with the Department of Public Welfare. In March 1973, the contract was transferred from the Junior League to Parents' and Children's Services. They agreed to assume responsibility for the administration of the program when it became apparent that direct Welfare Department control would be cumbersome and ineffective. The Junior League then began to withdraw gradually from the project. The League had certainly been a most effective catalyst in the establishment of the center and an able administrator during the inevitable first-year difficulties. It has continued to provide us with our most capable and dependable volunteers and a volunteer chairman to coordinate their activities.

Volunteers have been an integral part of our program since the beginning. Initially, all volunteers—twenty per week in two shifts per day—were provided by the Junior League. Before the center opened, they received training and general orientation by Shirley Bean of Parents' and Children's Services. The main objectives of the training session were to make people more aware of their own feelings about child abuse and of the effects these feelings might have on their ability to deal with the children. They were reminded that they would not be confronted with appallingly serious injuries at the time the children entered the center. Volunteers were led to recognize that everyone at one time or another feels angry enough to hurt a child, but that most people have sufficient strength to resist these feelings. Volunteers have to be able to empathize with the children's parents and understand their ambivalence toward their children.

We instituted monthly volunteer meetings to provide further training and communication between staff and volunteers. One of the League members wrote an excellent training manual which we use to orient new volunteers. The monthly meetings have proved to be very effective as a means of support for both staff and volunteers. Working with abused children can be frustrating and discouraging as well as exhilarating and satisfying. It is absolutely necessary to have a time when feelings can be aired, information shared, and reassurance offered. The need for open communication with volunteers cannot be stressed enough. One of our primary goals is to provide a consistent environment and routine for children who often come from chaotic homes. Consistency is impossible without cooperation of everyone involved.

Volunteers now come to us from a variety of sources, including area colleges, secondary schools, and community agencies, as well as the Junior League. One of our current problems is finding enough time and energy to recruit and screen new volunteers. Generally, volunteers fit into the program where they feel most comfortable. Some work with individual children, relating to them as might a special aunt or grandparent. Others float around the center filling in gaps where needed. Still others are willing to help with housekeeping and preparing meals. We have found volunteers to be valuable in providing a more objective view of children and in giving physical as well as emotional assistance to staff.

Another service the program provides is transportation. With families who are often isolated, depressed, and unmotivated, it is vital to reach out to them and bring the children to the center. We employ two women from the community who drive their own station wagons. Each car has an additional adult who holds infants, goes into homes, and maintains order in the car. These people are most valuable in building an ongoing relationship between families and the center. They also serve as a source of information for the social work staff. If the drivers encounter an unusual situation at home in the morning, theoretically the social worker can deal with it that same day.

Drivers cannot be hired on the basis of driving skills alone. They, too, must be warm, sympathetic people. They have to have incredible patience and sensitivity in difficult situations. One of our cars goes to a home where on three days out of five no one responds to the driver's presence. The family will not even wave out of a window if the children are not going. On several occasions these women have taken children home with them when their parents were not at home. One of the drivers calls two of the mothers on her route every morning to wake them up, so the children will be ready when the car arrives. The drivers also provide the children with additional responsible adults who care for them and about them in a consistent way.

The Inflicted Injury Unit is designated by law to receive all reports of child abuse in the Greater Boston Area. Nearly 90 percent of its referrals come from Boston City Hospital and the Children's Hospital Medical Center. The social worker usually meets the family while the child is hospitalized. The first decision is whether or not foster placement is necessary. With the establishment of the Gilday Center, the workers have an option other than foster placement or complete return of the child to his or her own home. The social workers have found that day care is a workable alternative for many families who feel overwhelmed by circumstances and isolated from the community. These families are tremendously relieved to have their children out of the home for the greater part of the day. "School" is an acceptable mode of social intervention. The workers often find that parents are less reluctant to see them once their relationship with the day care center is established. Both the worker and the center are available; both give to the parents as well as to the children.

We have been trying to create more parent involvement in the center. Day care staff are available as role models in parenting, but they must present themselves in a very non-threatening way. In the past, several mothers have spent many days with us. What was most noticeable was that they didn't want to participate in the program as aides, but as children. It was fascinating to watch a mother painting at the easel or swinging at the playground. On occasion, we have employed parents to ride on the daily routes. One of these mothers is now seriously trying to enroll in a training program for child care workers. In the fall, we had a party for parents. We were amazed that everyone came; they even mobilized enough to help each other with transportation. Currently, we are planning to start an informal, weekly afternoon get-together at the center for parents. It will be run by one of the child care workers and one of the social work staff.

Having a child in the day care center allows the social worker to keep a much closer watch on a family than would otherwise be possible. The child's behavior or appearance at the center is often an accurate barometer of the situation at home. One child's recurrent case of head lice indicates the level of her mother's depression. Another child's regression to an earlier mode of unacceptable behavior reflects a new crisis at home. Thus, the day care center provides the social worker with another means of establishing and maintaining a relationship with parents who are often elusive or intractable.

Our goals for children who attend the center can be described very briefly. We try to create both an atmosphere and environment which are consistent. The daily routine rarely varies, and children learn quickly that they can depend on it. Each child care worker is assigned four children as her primary responsibility. She tries to be a special person to each of these children, caring for them particularly at meals and nap time. Discipline is fair and appropriate. Children feel safe when they are not allowed to hurt themselves or others. Both anger and love are accepted. The center allows children to regress to behaviors which are normally unacceptable for their ages. We feed them, rock them, and hold them as if they were tiny babies. Somehow children know what behavior is appropriate at the center and what is appropriate at home, and they can act accordingly. We try to be honest about our feelings and verbalize them both for ourselves and for the children. We also encourage children to recognize other children's feelings and to verbalize rather than act out aggression. The best way to describe how our program works is through the progress of several children who have been enrolled at the center in the past.

David, age three and a half, has been attending the center for eleven months. When he first came, he was very shy, quiet, and nervous. He constantly twiddled his fingers and rocked back and forth. He talked very little and was difficult to understand. Occasionally he erupted into an attack on one of the younger children. He didn't respond to suggestions and remained inactive even at the playground. He seemed very tense and was unable to accept physical affection; all of his anxieties and anger remained locked inside him. After about three months, he began to get more aggressive and verbal. He swore at anyone who crossed him. His twiddling and other nervous habits began to disappear, and he became more affectionate. David also started to be more cooperative and broaden his range of activities. He really was able to express his anger verbally and move into a phase of almost frenetic activity. After about seven months, he gradually calmed down. Now we rarely hear him swear, and he plays with other children quite happily. At this point he is helpful and cooperative—a real leader in the group. He will move to a Headstart group within a few weeks.

Miguel came to us at age ten months. He was anemic and appeared to be retarded in his development. He was puny and apathetic. He wasn't crawling and had no experience with spoon feeding. Within a few weeks, he was babbling and crawling all over the place. He ate well and seemed interested in everything around him. He rocked himself when not getting attention from an adult. After a month at the center, Miguel could pull himself into a standing position, and he was smiling a lot. Soon he began taking a few steps with help, but, in the seven months he attended the center, he never walked independently. He refused to make the transition from baby food to table food. He always had minor scratches and bruises—probably the result of cramped living conditions with five siblings under age seven. Although his physical development continued to be slow, he grew into a bright, alert child who focused on people, smiled a lot, and explored toys and his environment appropriately. Finally, Miguel was placed in foster care as his mother continued to be overwhelmed by the other children and an extremely poor living situation. We saw him several months later and almost didn't recognize him. He had grown so much in every way!

Within five minutes of Scott's arrival at the center, he had soaked himself at the sink and stuck his head into the oven. He was incredibly active and attacked anyone who took something he was playing with. At two and a half he was talking, though not very clearly, and was interested in any and all activities. He was very curious and seemed quite bright. He often gave affection in a very aggressive way. When he had been with us for a month, we discovered he knew many letters from watching "Sesame Street" at home. He was able to participate in imaginative games and created many for himself. Scott needed constant attention to keep himself in control. Within three months, he was able to play by himself amid the group, but it was still difficult for him to be a part of the group. He had no interest in being held or comforted, but he began to give affection more gently. He reached the point of sitting still through lunch and asking adults for help or attention. After four months, he could play cooperatively with another child. Then he moved into a very aggressive phase in which he was once again on the verge of uncontrolled behavior almost constantly. A psychological evaluation was recommended to determine if medication might help his hyperactivity. At about the same time, the family situation became explosive, so Scott was placed in foster care temporarily. He made remarkable gains in self-control (without medication) in this home with a firm, but very warm, foster mother.

It is apparent from these descriptions that abused children share many common traits. What varies is at what point during a child's stay at the center these traits appear. David moved from nervousness and fear to hyperactivity and aggression to calmness and cooperation. Scott went from hyperactivity and aggression to relative calmness and cooperation, and then back to hyperactivity and aggression. We cannot offer any typical behavior or personality pattern which would fit every abused child, although we have certainly learned what kinds of behaviors to expect. For example: these children are much more apt to comfort an upset adult than to expect comfort when they are upset. They may be wary of physical contact of any kind. Their capacity for being "given to" is boundless. They show little or no distress at separation from parents. They can be very manipulative of adults from a very early age, and they are often accomplished actors. They sometimes respond negatively to praise as if it were safer to be "bad." They are generally reluctant to engage in any messy activities. Some seem highly skilled at provoking adults to anger, while others indiscriminately seek affection from any adult. Their language development is generally slow, and many have speech impediments. They demand immediate gratification and find it almost impossible to wait or take turns. Some are extremely well coordinated and others have little sense of body awareness. Initially, they seem completely without the normal childlike sense of joy.

As the program moves into its third year of existence, it continues to evolve and change. We are constantly faced with new problems and challenges. Some of the things we are currently struggling with include whether or not our three- to six-month limit on children's attendance is an effective or valuable goal. We are concerned with how to accommodate mothers who want to work without extending the staff's working hours. We worry about what happens to children and parents who have to make the transition to day care centers which provide less support. We are considering the possibility of establishing a follow-through center for children who turn three but probably couldn't handle a regular day care center. These and other issues insure that our work will never become dull or routine. We must keep re-evaluating our goals and methods and guard against convincing ourselves that we have all the answers.

23 Parents Anonymous: Reflections on the Development of a Self-Help Group

Cassie L. Starkweather,
S. Michael Turner, ACSW

Parents Anonymous is a national self-help organization which was established under the original name of "Mothers Anonymous" in 1970 by Jolly K., a 29-year-old mother who was desperate and angry because there was no immediate help to meet her needs. When asked by her therapist what she could do about this situation, she thought of starting a group composed of mothers with problems similar to hers.

Jolly K. had been living a "self-destructive" existence. Her own self-image was low, and she further confirmed this image by acts of child abuse and other asocial behavior. Thus, it was only with considerable support and encouragement that she could bring her idea to realization. Starting slowly with a few groups in California, Parents Anonymous (P.A.) has grown to some 90 chapters in the United States and Canada in 1974.

P.A. describes itself as a "crisis intervention program whose primary objective is to help prevent damaging relationships between parents and their children." P.A. offers its members two basic forms of help: (1) a weekly group meeting at which parents troubled about "losing their cool with their children" can share experiences and feelings and learn

151

to support as well as challenge each other; and (2) personal and telephone contact among members during periods of crisis. In many respects, it replicates the successful methods of Alcoholics Anonymous.

The appeal of P.A. no doubt results from the many inadequacies in our present ways of offering help to parents who abuse their children. The very fact that there seems to be a need for an anonymous organization strongly suggests the extent to which the problem is still viewed as a moral issue. Certainly, this attitude is reflected in many states' or localities' punitive practices in dealing with suspected child abuse. The second basis for its appeal lies in the openness and honesty among members, their easy accessibility during crises, and their feeling of urgency in finding concrete "do it now" approaches to dealing with their problems. This appeal strongly suggests some of the inadequacies of either non-directive pyschotherapeutic or so-called "authoritative" approaches which have been, almost universally, parents' only previous options in seeking help.

The idea of starting a Parents Anonymous Chapter in Boston took shape in the spring of 1972, after a visit to Boston by Dr. Ray Helfer, who was at that time writing his book *Helping the Battered Child and His Family.*[1] Dr. Helfer talked about Jolly K. with a good deal of enthusiasm for her work. At first we were somewhat intrigued by the idea, but we questioned how effective such a group might be. Nevertheless, we presented it at a Children's Advocates meeting and received approval to see what we could do about starting a chapter in Boston, under the auspices of Children's Advocates Committee on Resources. Fortified with the "Guidelines" from the parent chapter, we set about preparing publicity and exploring what similar groups were doing in this area. One person who was quite interested in starting the chapter was Mrs. Joan Wheeler, a nurse and a board member of Parents' and Children's Services, who had been active in that agency's "Parents' Center Project" and had also been instrumental in establishing the Gilday Center. On a trip to New York, Mrs. Wheeler spoke to Judge Bacon, who had started an independent chapter in New York; she brought back some material with her.

We decided the first job was to attract publicity. We wrote a number of stories for city-wide and local newspapers. We set up a target date of June 27, 1973, for the first meeting. Notices were sent out to all agencies that might have potential referrals.

The first few meetings were very disappointing; although we had received calls from many of the agencies inquiring about referring some of their clients, no more than two or three parents showed up at any

---

1. Kempe, C. H. and Helfer, R. E., eds. *Helping the Battered Child and His Family.* Philadelphia: Lippincott, 1972.

meeting. Parents would come to one meeting and then not return; new members would come instead. We also had several people who were so afraid that they either left in the middle of meetings or before the meeting even started, without finding out what was going to happen. It became clear to us that having more than one professional advisor at meetings was a real deterrent; obviously a parent who was interested in recruiting others and acting as organizer or chairman of a group would probably offer more effective leadership, at least until the chapter became strong enough to hold an election of officers.

In the fall of 1972, we received some very good publicity from a radio appearance and also from several newspaper articles. This exposure brought in at least a half dozen calls, and, although many were inappropriate for the focus of the group, we at least got our feet wet in the mass media. Still, things generally went along on the same sporadic level, until March of 1973 when Cassie S. learned about P.A. in a women's magazine. Cassie, who had recently had an incident of child abuse, felt that this organization would perhaps offer what she had been looking for. After benefitting from group therapy in a hospital setting, Cassie felt she needed the continuing support of a group situation. A social worker at Children's Hospital Medical Center referred her to a psychiatrist who was familiar with Children's Advocates' efforts to start a Boston P.A. chapter. It was through this referral that she became involved with P.A.

Both authors found the initial period of Cassie's leadership confusing. For one of us, it meant making the adjustment from being a "client" to that of group organizer; the other became an "advisor" instead of a sponsor.

Meetings under Cassie's leadership were at first quite difficult for her because of her lack of understanding of normal group process. She did not understand what was happening in sessions when the members would resist her as the group leader or when another group member would monopolize and compete with her for the role of leader. These experiences were frustrating until she received formal education in group process to learn that these phenomena would occur in any group—not necessarily in just a P.A. group. She became more confident when she became more understanding of the process.

Sporadic attendance continued to be a major problem. No two people ever seemed to appear at the same time; it was almost as though they were taking turns in order to avoid having to confront each other in the group. One member talked about everything possibly imaginable except her relationship with her children. A father was firmly convinced that the only way he could deal with his daughter's problem was with a baseball bat, and it seemed useless to attempt convincing him that he had other options.

Other members tested the group by making personal demands. One young wife deserted her husband during the period they were attending P.A.; the father called frantically, saying that he had to go to work and didn't have anybody to take care of the children. He wanted to know if he could bring the children to Cassie's house; he didn't know how to change diapers, the children hadn't been fed, and he wasn't sure what to give them. He was told he could bring the children over to Cassie's house and he would be helped to take care of them, but he would have to stay there with them—Cassie wasn't going to babysit, since that wasn't the purpose of P.A. He agreed to this, but the plan never materialized because his wife, who had been at a neighbor's home watching out the window, had seen him when he was leaving the house. Suddenly she reappeared to take care of the children.

Another young mother, whose child had only recently been returned from a foster home, decided it was time for her to start going out again as she felt very restricted and tied down. She wanted Cassie to take the baby for a weekend so she could go out with her boyfriend. Again, she was refused because it was felt that being with her child was something this mother needed to learn to cope with. Taking responsibility for group members' children poses quite a risk even though it may be demanded, because of the extreme ambivalence which underlies such requests.

When prospective members initially call to find out about the organization, the first thing they frequently ask is if we are going to take their children away from them. The second thing they ask is if we have a babysitting service.

We suspect that parents are concerned about losing their children because of their own ambivalent feelings about them. We have explored this possibility and learned that they feel they have either abused or mistreated their children so badly that they don't deserve to have them. In this respect, it has been our experience that most parents judge themselves more harshly than other more objective people tend to judge them. The fear of losing their children frequently diminishes with reassurance from other members that they are not the monsters they think they are.

Generally speaking, P.A. members are so afraid they are going to be judged by others as harshly as they judge themselves that they are afraid to go out and seek help. Frequently our members express fears of dealing with a professional person, seeing differences in education, sex, or social status as basic differences that would prevent easy communication or mutual understanding.

Members express feelings of gratification at finding that other parents are "in the same boat." They contrast this with their feelings about professionals who, they often assume, have not taken out the time from their training and current job responsibilities to raise families of their own.

One parent recounted a particularly poignant example of this:

> My initial experience was a fearful one. The psychiatrist who, to the best of my knowledge, would determine whether or not my child would be returned to me seemed rather cold and clinical, wearing a white coat. I knew that when I went to see him, I would have to be able to convince him and reassure him that bringing the child home was the best thing for everybody concerned—and that in the future I would be able to foresee and prevent the child abuse situation that had occurred before. When I sat down at his office, I was really scared. I didn't want to talk to him; I just wanted to get up and leave.
>
> At this particular time, his telephone rang, and he received a call which I assumed was from his wife because of the feedback he was giving on the phone. When he hung up the phone, he was visibly upset; he told me that all of his children (and he had five) had chicken pox at the same time. He was frantic about who was going to take care of them and how everything was going to get done. He expressed the fact that he was concerned about the youngsters being sick. I could relate to these concerns, and I could relate to him as a father—I had looked around his office, and I'd seen pictures of kids that obviously were his. I then felt more comfortable speaking with him about myself. I felt he would be more understanding than the psychiatrist I had seen before who had spent 14 years at school, didn't have children, and admitted to me that—other than what was mandatory in her schooling—she hadn't ever really babysat. There were situations that I tried to discuss with her, and I almost got the feeling that she was avoiding talking about these things because she felt very uncomfortable.

We recognize that often this fear of professionals serves as a smokescreen for a parent's difficulty in admitting the problem to himself. P.A. members handle such difficulties by sharing their own similar feelings and experiences. The keynote here is honesty and directness. The term "abuse" is used liberally at meetings until it becomes a part of a member's everyday vocabulary. Our goal is to help parents admit the fact that they are abusive and accept the fact. Only then can they begin to cope with an abuse problem. It would be easy to say, "Hell, this kid deserves it; he sets himself up for a beating; he won't go to sleep until he gets a beating." It is easier for parents to think that their children are getting only what they justly deserve, rather than accept their share of the problem. Our insistence on frankness has a healthy affect: parents find that they are relieved. Nothing in their prior experience has led them to expect to find anyone able to accept an abusive parent for what he or she is. They expect rejection; because of this expectation, they beat around the bush, never use the right words, and gloss over what is actually happening. P.A. doesn't pull any punches; they actually say why they're beating this kid and challenge each other to do something about it. The members are offered an opportunity not only to share their experiences but to share alternatives and to help set up a definite plan concerning an individual's needs.

In this way we provide not only the open admission—and the relief that this gives—that you don't have to hide from something the rest of society finds difficult to stomach; but we also give some very concrete ways of helping parents to cope better with the feeling once it hits them.

Out of their own experiences, members set about helping each other recognize that certain situations can lead up to abusive episodes. A mother may be helped to realize that when she is broke and it's two days before check-day, it's not a good time to take the kids window-shopping because she's going to be beset with the "gimme's" and the "I want's." If she can avoid the stores and avoid the toy departments under these circumstances, it may prevent her from belting the kids and taking something off the counter.

One mother reported that it took her a long time to recognize the danger signs. She said when she felt physically tight and tense early in the morning, that would be the kind of day in which she would be apt to take it out on her children. She learned to make alternative plans for herself and her children on such days. Another mother told the group that she was able to re-channel and reconstruct her day according to how she felt in given situations in order to avoid a crisis. However, if things went wrong and a crisis did erupt, she was more likely to cope with it because she could expect that in the course of the P.A. meeting, somebody was going to ask her casually, "How did your week go?" Just thinking about what her answer would be—and knowing it would be difficult to pretend with other parents—was an important factor in controlling her abusive behavior.

Even though the Boston Chapter of P.A. is still struggling through its infancy, we feel we have learned some things of value to others interested in starting a similar venture. Following are some of our thoughts.

1. *Use of information and guidelines from the Parent Chapter.* We found the help provided by national's "Guidelines" invaluable. However, in utilizing these guidelines, we realized they must be adapted to suit local conditions. One of the first difficulties we encountered at our meetings resulted from the fact that the guidelines are very oriented to California's abuse laws. The Massachusetts laws are not necessarily more liberal, but they are different. More support and more acceptance are given to parents in Massachusetts—more referrals are made to helping agencies. It's a lot more difficult to have a child taken away in Massachusetts than it is in California, so people probably are not as inhibited about asking for help here. We therefore recommend familiarity with child abuse laws in one's own state and adaptation of the National Guidelines to the local situation.

2. *The Role of the Professional Advisor.* A Parents Anonymous leader needs professional help in three areas: (1) aid enabling the leader to attain a degree of objectivity, which is necessary if the group is to be helpful; (2) knowledge about the resources available to help people outside P.A.; and (3) technical knowledge about how to lead the group itself so that meetings can be productive.

It can be very frustrating for a lay leader to deal with group phenomena with which he or she is not familiar. Frequently the leader can feel overwhelmed and overinvolved with what's happening in the group or with family situations. Sound advice from professionals in a consultative position is helpful, if not absolutely necessary—if for no other reason than to permit the leader to vent personal frustrations.

Despite the trials of the Boston Chapter, we are optimistic about its potential. We are planning to expand and become more available to people; frequently mothers who call and say they are very interested in attending P.A. meetings, or who have been referred to the group, aren't able to come at the given time. Eventually we will have to have both a daytime and an evening group. We will need to develop an outreach program. We don't think we have reached more than a handful of potential members or referral sources, but it is our intention to increase our efforts with the help of Children's Advocates, Inc., so that we can make P.A. help available to as many as need it.

PART SEVEN

THE LAW

24 The Law and Child Abuse

Arthur H. Rosenberg,
LLM, JD

The problems of the abused or neglected child and his family are not the exclusive province of a single profession or group—be it law, medicine, nursing, social work, or psychiatry. They are problems which have a multiplicity of aspects and which are often, therefore, most responsive to and require the combined skills of many professionals and paraprofessionals. Unfortunately, the use of a multi-disciplinary approach has commonly been impeded by the failure of individual professions to recognize beneficial skills and techniques of other disciplines. The tendency has been "to go it alone," to deny the possible benefits of assistance from other quarters, with each group tending to view these problems from its own narrow perspective and to consider its approach as wholly adequate. Accordingly, treatment plans for such cases frequently neither consider nor fully utilize all available resources; services are often of limited scope, and they tend not to be of maximum efficacy in terms of either treatment of the present injury or protection against future harm.

During the past few years, it has been my good fortune to work as an attorney in a number of contexts and with a variety of professional and paraprofessional groups on the problems of the abused and neglected child. My experiences in the field have convinced me that there exists a significant lack of information and misunderstanding among all groups —including courts and lawyers—about the legal issues involved in this delicate work. For example, among concerned non-lawyers there is an urgent need for legal consultation to provide both accurate information about the laws and an accurate understanding of those laws, if the objectives of a legislative approach are to be achieved. Equally important, there is an urgent, almost wholly unmet need for legal consultation at the clinical level, when legal issues, possible legal action, and their consequences must be considered in the formulation of a treatment plan, in the decision-making process, and in the implementation of those decisions.

For courts and lawyers, there is an equivalent need for education, not only about the statutory law, but about actual practice and the need for inter-disciplinary approach. The inter-disciplinary approach has been used no more by the legal profession than by other involved groups. Yet the need for such an approach is often unmistakably clear in the juvenile law area and, most especially, in the child protection area. The majority of lawyers have little occasion to be involved in such cases and to develop an expertise—partly because of the infrequency of requests for their assistance by other involved groups, the relatively few cases which reach the courts, and the few opportunities for practice in the field. Consequently, among lawyers and non-lawyers there is a discomfort and an unfamiliarity with their proper role in such proceedings. This discomfort is underscored by a limited or confused understanding of the applicable law itself, its consequences, and its goals. Additionally, members of both groups notably lack appreciation of the other's role, as well as the means by which the skills and expertise of the other involved groups may be utilized. Because of this lack of information or even misinformation about legal issues, and the inability to clarify roles among lawyers and non-lawyers alike, valuable resources for protecting children are often misused or unavailable. Thus is precluded maximum, effective intervention in cases which often involve serious risk of death or bodily injury. This chapter considers some of the difficulties of coping with child abuse from a purely legal viewpoint and seeks thereby to minimize inappropriate expectations of the legal system and suggest possible realistic benefits to be derived from it.

Every state in the United States has statutory laws about child abuse. Although differing in both form and substance, such statutes commonly are aimed at two distinct but related functions: first, to compel reporting of injuries; second, to provide a protective response. No state lacks a statute to cause the reporting of a variety of forms of what may be defined by that particular state's statute as either child abuse or child neglect. Similarly, no state lacks a statute to authorize the initiation of protective action either coincidental to reporting or in situations not encompassed by the mandatory reporting provision.

Every state has an agency or agencies authorized to receive those reports—usually social welfare agencies, but also law enforcement officials in some states. Still further, no state in the country lacks a legal forum to hear such cases and to provide protection; whether or not there exists or should exist other types of service is an altogether different issue which depends upon one's view of the role of the court. The extent to which services are available, the nature of such services, and the issue of who is to provide them also vary.

To put it another way, every state, to various degrees, has a legal framework to encourage case findings, to mobilize protective action, to formulate a treatment plan, and to provide supervision and services in these cases. Yet we know from available statistics that, while the incidence of child abuse and neglect continues to rise at an alarming rate, reporting and court action tend to be negligible. This situation occurs despite legislative action aimed at expanding both the types of reportable injuries and the categories of persons mandated to make such reports, and, further, despite legislation expanding immunity from liability and abrogating limitations of confidentiality and/or privileged communication. That is not necessarily to say that, absent of increased reporting and court action, such cases are not being serviced by both public and private agencies or individual practitioners. Still, it is reasonable to expect that, with a growing incidence of abuse and neglect and the availability of improved reporting statutes, the incidence of reported cases and the number of court actions should also increase. This has not happened: whatever action has or has not been taken with regard to these cases, legal requirements and options are for the most part being ignored.

The statistics in Massachusetts offer a typical example of this situation. Using the data of the 1965 study conducted by the National Opinion Research Center Survey, it has been estimated that Massachusetts would have approximately 40,000 child abuse and neglect cases annually. A survey conducted in 1971 by the Massachusetts Governor's Committee on Child Abuse set the figure, more realistically, at approximately 7,290 cases in this state per year.

In contrast to those figures, the number of cases reported to the Massachusetts Department of Public Welfare—the agency exclusively mandated by statute to receive reports—shows how woefully infrequently the reporting mechanism is employed. The Massachusetts Department of Public Welfare indicates a total of 220 cases reported from three major cities in 1972, 205 cases reported from those same three cities in 1973, and a gross total of 329 cases reported in the entire state in 1973.

164

Regardless of which of the two estimates one chooses to adopt, it is clear that reporting is minimal. The total cases reported in 1973 constitute less than 5 percent of the latter estimate and slightly more than three quarters of 1 percent of the former estimate. Similarly, statistics from the district courts of Massachusetts also reflect that a minimal number of complaints of child abuse and neglect were brought to the courts. The total figure reported for 1972 was 529 and for 1973, 523 cases. The four juvenile courts of Massachusetts report that in 1972, 252 care and protection petitions were brought to seek court intervention, not only for protection, but also for services to children subjected to various harms and risks of harm. In 1973, the available statistics indicate that 247 care and protection petitions were brought in those same courts.

These figures, typical also of those in other states, reflect a persistent, chronic failure of compliance with the mandatory reporting statutes and a minimal usage of available statutes designed to provide protective intervention on behalf of children. The precise reasons for this situation are unclear. In part, it may be due to a willingness to deny and repress the problems of child abuse and/or neglect. It may also be due to negligence in failing to diagnose properly child abuse and/or neglect where they may be, in fact, the presenting problem. In either event, there would be no reporting or other action taken.

Worse still, the reporting failure may be attributable to a situation in which there is both recognition and diagnosis of the problem, followed by a willful and total disregard not only of the legal duty to report, but of a moral and professional obligation to pursue legal protection and provide care. Again, this disregard may result from the pervasive ignorance as well as misunderstanding of the laws and their consequences. The requirement of reporting is, if not unknown to many of those persons who fall within its purview, often ignored by those persons mandated to report.

Without excusing their failure to report, it has certainly been the unfortunate experience of many seeking to honor this duty that reporting does not lead to services or, at best, leads to inadequate services. Much of the same is true for those who do seek to avail themselves of legal remedies. For such persons, the legal system is an unpleasant, unfamiliar prospect to consider and—perhaps even more appropriate—an unlikely context within which to pursue "helpful" medical and social services. Additionally, the failures to report and/or take court action may also be due to a situation in which a public or private agency has already assumed the responsibility for both protective as well as supportive services. In such cases, once services are being provided, there seems little reason, other than a purely legal one—compliance with a statutory requirement—to initiate a report to the designated agency, especially if that agency is known to be ineffectual or unable to provide similar services.

If law enforcement agencies are among the report recipients, case reporting might lead to criminal action, which is not usually seen as therapeutic by the types of persons usually obligated to make these reports—that is, physicians, social workers, nurses, etc. Certainly no need for court action would exist if satisfactory compliance is made with the treatment plan by the parents or caretakers and some assurance is given that no risk to the child exists. Under such circumstances, reporting seems to be of no real practical value; it is likely only to imperil the therapeutic relationship while at the same time jeopardizing the privacy of the family.

Whatever then might be the precise cause for these failures of compliance and usage, if the statistic estimates of child abuse and neglect have the slightest validity, those persons—professionals and nonprofessionals alike—required to report by the statutes of all fifty states not only violate the law by their inaction but, more importantly, fail those children for whose benefit these statutes were intended.

From the legal viewpoint, much of the work of the past ten years has been directed toward the passage initially of child abuse reporting statutes and the gradual refinement of those same statutes in order to enhance reporting. As described by DeFrancis et al. (*Child Abuse Legislation in the 1970's,* American Human Association, Revised Edition, 1974)

> . . . the more significant patterns noted were:
> – the broadening of the base of those who are mandated to report;
> – a movement toward enlarging the concept of reportable abuse;
> – a reduction in the number of states with permissive rather than mandatory reporting laws;
> – an increase in the number of states designating the state or county department of social services as receiving agencies for abuse reports;
> – an increase in the number of states mandating the establishment of central registries.

Undoubtedly, some of these refinements will initially increase reporting—expanding the numbers of persons required to report and the definitions of reportable harm cannot fail to have some impact upon the numbers of reported cases. What then? What will be achieved in the long run if these changes occur without the additional human services or manpower being provided, if there still exists ignorance or misunderstanding of the substantive laws, their scope, and their objectives, or if there is a continued failure to recognize the effective limits of legislation per se. A continued, increased disillusionment with the reporting requirement and the legal process is the very least outcome to be anticipated.

If we are to avoid the frustrations of the past and the perceived—if not actual—failure of the legal system to contribute appropriately to these problems, we must appreciate what it is that our reporting and protective legislation can reasonably achieve. Having unrealistic expectations of the legal system—both the laws themselves and the courts—to ameliorate problems of child abuse and neglect are as bad as having no expectations of benefit and turning away from a valuable resource. On the basis of reporting and court statistics, our legislative efforts of the past ten years have created a false or at least an unrealistic expectation of remediation. The heavy emphasis on newer and better legislation has—whether intentionally or inadvertently—misled many into a belief that, with proper statutes, these problems might be solved or controlled. Instead, it appears that the job of child protection has indeed not been well done, that the problem remains largely unresolved, and that the efforts to enact better statutory laws have usurped major commitments of time and energy—which might well have been better invested in developing or delivering needed services.

To a great extent, the problems of dealing with child abuse through legislation and the legal system stem from the lack of a consistent philosophy toward children and toward families and toward objectives which we might seek to pursue. There is no weaker area of the law than that area which relates to the family and its members and to the relationship of the family to third parties. The conflict between parents and children in all dimensions is reflected in conflicting legal views of the reciprocal rights and duties of parents and children. The inadequacy and confusion of the laws governing the subject reflect our own ambivalence about our children and ourselves as parents.

Expansion of the legal rights of children is often seen by parents as a diminution of their authority; where there are clearly defined rights, there are correlative duties. To establish the child's right to sound physical and mental health is to define the parents' duty. To establish the parents' duty is to define a level of performance, however minimal, as a basis for judging adequacy and perhaps for finding failure. On this basis, other third parties—be they human service agencies or courts—assess parents' performance and hold them accountable.

The result of this ambivalence is the failure to develop a consistent philosophy to guide in the formulation of effective legislation. On the one hand, we favor protection of the child; on the other hand, we cleave to sustaining family integrity, often at all costs. These are not always consistent alternatives. Consequently, we fail to commit the resources necessary to make such legislation either meaningful or workable and thereby fail to garner the maximum preventive or remedial benefits contemplated by the laws. Having recognized the problem and dignified it with legislation, most states consider the job well done and the problem solved.

It would appear, however, from the rising tide of child abuse and neglect in this country, that the result of our inability to resolve the ambivalence and to commit the necessary resources has been to perpetuate the perception of legislation per se as the panacea for such problems. Unfortunately, this perception is quite consistent with efforts in other areas. Legislation has been similarly employed to deal with problems of violent behavior, sexual deviance, drug abuse, and public drunkenness —often without additional resources for coping with such issues. Past legislative failures in these areas demonstrate clearly that such problems cannot be legislated away and that our courts, all too often the forum for action, lack the skills to effectuate remediation.

This is not to say, however, that legislation for dealing with such problems could not be useful, or that it would not be useful regarding child abuse and neglect. Legislation can be useful. However, good legislation can only contribute to the solution of such problems; legislation alone cannot solve those problems. The failure to recognize this ultimate reality dooms into ineffectuality what often could be achieved by good legislation.

In the context of child abuse, for example, it must be recognized that the existence of a child abuse reporting law, or a law prohibiting child abuse, or even a law establishing child abuse as a criminal offense, cannot control such behavior. Situations exist in which such behavior is not susceptible to legislative control: where the behavior derives from the emotional disorder of a parent or caretaker; where the behavior derives from the personal belief of such a person—be it a religious belief, a philosophical belief, or a belief in the merits of corporal punishment; where poor judgement, negligence, inexperience, or immaturity of responsible parties results in harm to the child; and where harm results from mental illness, uncontrollable behavior, or an irrational state of mind. In addition to these situations, laws cannot effectively curb behavior when its roots are steeped in poverty, the acceptibility of violence as a lifestyle, and the overwhelming despair of life itself. In such cases, the objectives of realistic legislation must be limited, and our expectations of the law must be limited. Law is unlikely to control or perhaps even prevent the initial incident arising directly from such causes. The law can only encourage identification of such situations. Once situations are identified, however, good legislation can help to establish limits on future behavior, can provide protection, and can offer the framework within which other disciplines may operate.

Recent legislation regarding alcoholism, drug treatment, children in need of services, and mental health reflects such thinking. The passage, existence, or operation of law is in itself not the end, but rather the beginning of an effort to address a particular problem. These new laws assume that the legal system and laws can encourage, mobilize, and support the activities of other professionals with skills and resources which are not within the repertoire of the legal system itself. This is a new legislative direction. It recognizes that the traditional outcome of both the civil and criminal law—money damages, fines, restitution of property, injunctive relief, and/or imprisonment—are not relevant to the resolution of such problems. The focus is, therefore, not on a proscription and punishment of the behaviors to be curtailed, but rather on definition of such behaviors and development of the mechanisms which will lead to relevant, humane responses by community resources.

In addition to the more therapeutic objectives of recent legislation, there is a second and more traditional view of the objectives of legislation—that is, that a good law can also proscribe the limits of acceptable conduct. Underlying this concept of law is the notion that, where there exists the capability to appreciate limits and to conform one's conduct, a good law can be preventive and can preclude the initial incident. However, without such capability to conform one's conduct and/or without understanding of the limits of acceptable behavior, it is unrealistic to expect the law to control such behavior. Many of the precipitants leading to child abuse and neglect are precisely those not subject to being controlled effectively by legislative proscription. While we may still wish to proscribe such conduct by legislation, we must recognize the probable failure of such an approach for dealing with this particular problem.

In order then to have a good law which obtains its objectives as being either preventive or remedial, there must be both a philosophical context and a commitment to achieve specific objectives in pursuance of that philosophy. Without articulation of a philosophy and without a clear understanding of objectives, there cannot be a consistent, rational scheme for implementation: without such a scheme, legislation is meaningless.

At best, the existing reporting and protection statutes of the various states are expressions of community concern and reflections of certain values. Few if any are truly effective in either a preventive or remedial manner; few if any are clearly directed to either or both of those objectives. In a global sense, these statutes indicate that such conduct, however ill-defined, is not condoned by our society. The existence of such statutes indicates some intention that protective action on behalf of our children is needed.

Implicitly underlying the need for such action is the assumption that there are limits on permissible behavior by parents or other caretakers toward children. Similarly underlying all of the various statutes is the assumption that third parties—often the state, through its courts or public welfare agencies—have the duty and/or the right to intervene in the family and that the physical and emotional well-being of children is of sufficient concern to the state to justify intervention. It remains to be seen, however, whether the new legislation of the 1970's—arising out of a need to deal with these problems more effectively than antecedent laws, being more resolute in favor of protecting the child and more committed to third party intervention, and containing more specific and realistic objectives—will better insure the rights of our children to sound physical health, mental health, security, and well-being. The potential for such an achievement clearly exists within such laws. However, the extent to which we achieve these goals will, for the most part, be determined by the means that we adopt to implement the legislation. A continued ignorance about, misunderstanding of, or denial of the legal aspects of these problems will surely not lead in the right direction.

25 Child Abuse and the Central Registry

Gail Garinger, Attorney
James N. Hyde

Much national attention has been directed in recent months to the issues of confidentiality, data banks, and the right of privacy of citizens; yet, little dialogue has occurred regarding the relevance of these issues to the establishment (and operation of) state-wide central registries of abused/neglected children—despite the fact that more than forty states in the United States have created such central registries either by statute or administrative aegis. This chapter is designed to explore the potential benefits/costs inherent in the concept of a central registry identifying abused/neglected children.

Most experts in the child abuse field view a central registry as serving the following three main functions:

1. Ascertaining the true incidence and nature of child abuse/neglect

2. Assisting professionals/courts to determine whether or not a particular child has been abused/neglected

3. "Keeping track" of abusive/neglectful parents who are prone to "hospital/agency shopping"

Thus, the central registry in most states is designed to act both as a central warehouse for statistical data to be used for research purposes and as a practical tool for assisting professionals involved in day-to-day child abuse case management.

In addition to serving the above three functions, however, a central registry is seen by some professionals as a first and necessary step in the tracking of individuals who are prone to antisocial behavior. Persons such as Dr. Vincent Fontana, in his recent book *Somewhere a Child is Crying*,[1] hypothesize a causal connection between child abuse and subsequent antisocial conduct. A central registry is, therefore, a means for isolating potential deviants so that they can be treated prior to the commission of deviant acts.

The information recorded in the central registry varies from state to state, but at a minimum such data usually include the following: name and address of child believed to be abused/neglected; child's sex and age; names and addresses of child's parents or caretakers; nature and extent of injuries; and evidence of prior abuse/neglect.

Provisions regarding access to the information in the central registry also differ among the states. However, very few states provide specific statutory guidelines delineating who shall have access to the information in the central registry or the procedures for gaining and protecting such access. Instead, a typical state statute reads as follows:

> Data and information relating to individual cases in the central registry shall be confidential and shall be made available only with the approval of the commissioner or upon court order. The commissioner shall establish rules and regulations governing the availability of such data and information. (Massachusetts General Laws, Chapter 1076 Acts of 1973, Section 51F).

This blanket provision for confidentiality, even when taken together with a mandate to a state agency to promulgate appropriate regulations, provides little statutory protection for the suspected parent/caretaker. Such a conclusion is even more likely, given the absence in most state statutes of specific substantive and procedural safeguards for the suspected parent/caretaker.

Specific problems which exist at present, given the broad and somewhat vague child abuse statutes in most states, include the following:

1. Central registries often include cases of *suspected* abuse as well as cases of proven abuse/neglect. Yet, parents are usually (a) not in-

---

1. Fontana, V. F. *Somewhere a Child is Crying: The Maltreatment Syndrome.* New York: Macmillan, 1973.

formed that their names are being put on the list, (b) not informed of the criteria which are utilized in making the decision to put names on the list, and (c) not given the right or opportunity to challenge their names being put on the list.

2. The criteria for specifying those who may enter the name of a child or his family in such a registry are exceedingly broad.

3. As was mentioned previously, right of access to information in the central registry is a grave problem.

4. Usually no statutory provisions govern the time period that a name should remain listed in the central registry. Issues such as the criteria for removal of a name from the registry and the automatic expungement of information after a certain time interval have not been resolved.

In addition to these problems, central registries of child abuse/neglect cases raise all of the concerns which pertain in general to computerized data banks and the right of privacy. The fear that central registries can become "maniacal vacuum cleaners," sucking in the names of children and parents and feeding this information to other state agencies, credit bureaus, insurance companies, and the F.B.I. should not be taken lightly. Such a consideration is not implausible, especially considering the hypothesis advanced by some that the abused children of today become the criminals of tomorrow.

The case which follows attempts to explore some of the implications that the use of a child abuse registry may have in acting as a substitute for an adequate data base in arriving at management decisions concerning potential cases of child abuse. The danger of predicating action on inadequate or incomplete information has serious implications not only for the child but the family as well. The mechanism that is set into motion once a diagnosis of abuse has been made is exceedingly difficult to stop; it may in fact result in the transformation of a question of a family's ability to protect a child into a self-fulfilling prophecy.

CASE PRESENTATION

In January, 1972, Mrs. Smith brought her son Robert into the emergency room at Baker General Hospital in Boston. She had recently moved to the Boston area from New York State with her husband and two children and had not as yet found a pediatrician or health center to provide for her family's medical care. She and her husband had decided to move to Boston when her husband lost his job as a welder in the town where they had lived. Mrs. Smith had a sister living in Boston, and they both felt that her husband might have a better chance of finding a job in a large urban area.

Things had gone badly for the Smiths from the start. Mr. Smith had not been able to find a job, and the small amount of savings they had managed to amass was gone after a short time. Mr. Smith was able to collect unemployment benefits, but it was hardly enough to cover his family's expenses. Although they were living with Mrs. Smith's sister, relations were becoming strained with the two families crammed into a four room apartment.

When Mrs. Smith arrived at the emergency room she looked tired and haggard. She explained that recently Robert, who was eight months old, had become irritable and cranky and that he wasn't feeding well. The physician who examined the child found an infant who appeared normal developmentally, although clearly dirty and in need of a bath. The physical exam was otherwise unremarkable, except that Robert did appear to have some difficulty breathing. The doctor decided to have a skeletal survey done. The films showed a small hairline fracture of one of the right ribs.

Mrs. Smith was questioned by the physician about what might have caused the injury to Robert. She seemed vague and defensive, citing one or two minor incidents that had occurred in the last several weeks. The examining physician was puzzled by this explanation and voiced his suspicion to Mrs. Smith that the injury might have been inflicted. The mother immediately broke down and cried, explaining all of the difficulties she and her husband had encountered in the last several weeks, but vehemently denying having caused the injury. Although Mrs. Smith was subsequently sent home with Robert, the doctor indicated to her that he wanted her to return for follow-up in three days and to be seen by one of the hospital's social workers.

Mrs. Smith did not return for the follow-up visit and all efforts to contact her failed. The Smith's name, however, was reported to the state-wide central registry.

Two years later Mrs. Smith's daughter, Elizabeth, was brought to Claire Hospital with a serious leg injury. Mrs. Smith explained that her daughter had been playing down in the basement of their new house while she was upstairs putting the two-year-old to bed. Apparently, the child had climbed up on a table which had turned over, pinning Elizabeth underneath it.

On examination the child appeared frightened and withdrawn. X-rays revealed no broken bones, but the child had sustained considerable trauma to the leg. The physician was suspicious because the mother seemed exceedingly defensive and nervous while Elizabeth was being examined. He gently explored the possibility of an inflicted injury, and Mrs. Smith became angry and hostile. A quick check of the central registry revealed that Mrs. Smith's son, Robert, had been seen two years ago at Baker General Hospital with an injury of suspicious origin. Although the injury might well have been treated at home, the mother's outburst as well as the previous history of suspected inflicted injury aroused sufficient concern on the part of the doctor that he decided that he had better admit Elizabeth until a more thorough assessment could be done of the home situation by the hospital's social service department.

Hearing of the doctor's decision to admit Elizabeth, Mrs. Smith refused to consent to the admission, saying that she could not understand why her daughter had to be admitted if she could just as well be treated as an outpatient.

The physician, feeling ever more anxious and concerned, secured a court order through the hospital's attorney to have Elizabeth held pending a hearing on the matter the following day in Juvenile Court.

The management of this case and, in particular, the role of the Central Registry in determining the response of a physician to the family in crisis raises a number of important legal and clinical management issues. What, for example, were the criteria used by the physician to report the Smith family in the first place? Did the physician at Baker General have an obligation to inform the family that they were being reported to the Central Registry, and if so, should the family have had access to the report of any subsequent evaluation/investigation carried out by the Welfare Department?

Of further concern is the whole issue of expungement. Should reports be allowed to languish in the Welfare Department files, if reports are not substantiated, and if a period of time—say two years, as in this case—elapses without further incident? Who should have access to reports, and should evidence of reports made in the past serve as the major criterion for initiating legal action in the absence of adequate data base? Finally, and perhaps the most difficult question of all, did the availability of the Central Registry facilitate or complicate the management of this case?

The hypothetical case that has been presented is purposefully not one of clear-cut abuse; but, neither is it atypical. In an area where diagnosis is so often based on a subjective reading of incomplete data, cases such as that of the Smith family are not uncommon. The trend in child abuse legislation across the country has been to build in the central registry concept as an aid to the diagnostic process and as a method of identifying high-risk children. So long as the process implicit in the existence of child abuse registries continues to stigmatize families —as opposed to insuring the delivery of adequate and appropriate services—the role and function of these data management systems must be carefully scrutinized.

PART EIGHT

COMMUNICATION

26 The Development of Children's Advocates, A Community Approach

Deborah A. Hill, MSW

Helpful communication can pave the way toward successful inter-agency services. Poor communication, or no communication, can thwart the helping process or even exert a negative influence. It is ironic that the area of protective services, which requires such complex input from cooperating agencies, sometimes suffers the most from disjointed, fragmented services which drain the energy and spirit of those trying to help. Feelings of anger and frustration found in those interagency contacts where one agency feels another is not doing its job or is not sharing necessary or helpful information are only exaggerated and heightened in the area of protective work where anxieties are normally high.

Other communities have expressed interest in obtaining information about how we minimized some of this frustration through the formation of an interagency group. In Boston, with its unusually high number of competitive teaching hospitals and its many social agencies, both old and new, our task of communication and coordination was not a simple one. Our first efforts at organization were born out of the desperate need for better communication which may be found in any community, large or small.

Out of these feelings of frustration and helplessness—but also feelings of conviction that something could be done—a few professionals began meeting informally together to work on communication difficulties between the referring hospital and the protective agency. This small group, representing one hospital and one, then two, protective agencies, grew gradually into what is now Children's Advocates, Inc., an enthusiastic multidisciplinary group composed of twenty-three agencies concerned with providing services to families of abused children.

As the group has developed, not only have communication problems been addressed, but other important things have taken place as well. Through a sharing of a given agency's function and problems, other agencies come to know what services that agency can and cannot provide and how best those services can be obtained for a family. The hospital and private agency come to know better what to expect from the public agency and how to describe most realistically and helpfully its function to a family. Hospitals and private agencies learn how they can play a preventative role and assume the major treatment role in certain families, with the public agency providing a back-up or collaborative role.

Children's Advocates has grown out of both practical and emotional needs. The fact that abusing parents run to a multitude of health facilities and agencies means that cooperation by all is needed to identify and treat children and families at risk. The fact that abusing and neglectful families require a multitude of services—medical, counseling, legal, monetary, educational, day care, housing—means that a variety of professional and nonprofessional disciplines must work cooperatively together.

As important as an agency's need for the practical help of another agency is its need for emotional support in dealing with a problem of this magnitude. Just as on a personal level, sharing lightens burdens, so it is in a group. Feelings of anger, frustration, and helplessness are channeled into constructive work. Member agencies have come to the group with varying degrees of experience and expertise. Members have learned from each other about how to identify problems, how to intervene, and how and where to refer in a helpful way. Hospital delegates have shared their ideas on the values and pitfalls of a vulnerable-child list, as well as on the mechanical aspects of providing information while insuring confidentiality. They have also shared information on how their particular hospital develops and utilizes a trauma team and what the problems are in this process. There has been an increasing trend to add consultants from the protective agencies to the individual hospital trauma teams. This has done much to improve family care.

All agency delegates work together on committees of their choice toward developing additional resources to service families. The Children's Advocates education committee formed its goals in response to serious concerns over widespread failure to report actual cases of child abuse—failure on the part of hospitals or agencies to recognize warning signs and offer preventative help and failure of knowledgeable social agencies to assume their responsibility in treatment, rather than adopting a "hands-off" attitude toward any problem that hinted of abuse or neglect. The committee's work has involved sponsorship of symposia as well as development of a speaker's bureau.

The resource committee is composed of delegates who want to do something about the inadequacy of services available to abusing families. They have arranged for a telephone service to respond to calls from the lay and professional communities asking for information or referral. They have sponsored a local self-help group called Parents' Anonymous; they are helping it through its growing pains as it seeks to find and encourage new members. The resource committee has struggled with the pros and cons of a vulnerable child list and its proper management.

The public relations committee arose out of the need to acquaint the public with the nature of child abuse problems and to inform people of what can be done, what is being done, and what their individual responsibilities are. They published a brochure designed to encourage families to seek help.

Opportunities which were developed to present programs on both radio and television served both to educate the public and encourage parents to seek help. This method was clearly productive. In addition, the *Boston Globe* has given broad coverage of an educational nature on the problems of abuse-neglect at the times of the symposia and at other times.

The legal issues committee developed out of concern for the obvious need for education on the part of court clerks and judges who must make critical decisions affecting children and families, often with little or no background as to the issues and problems involved. Handling of these cases varies widely from court to court, within even a small geographic area; often, responsible worried parties hesitate to seek needed court involvement out of fear their request will be denied and they will lose what trust their family has in them. This committee is seeking opportunities to provide helpful programs in court settings. Because our charter declares us a nonprofit organization, we cannot lobby in support of particular legislation. However, we can and do provide information and opinions when asked by groups preparing legislation.

Another group of members has seen the need for a practice committee to study individual case management issues and to explore and learn from their own cases what has proved helpful to families.

Lastly, a small membership committee talks with those agencies interested in joining Children's Advocates and evaluates whether or not the prospective agency's goals and those of Children's Advocates are the same and whether or not we can contribute to the functioning of one another. One criterion for membership is that the agency or individual considered be directly involved in providing service to families where neglect and abuse are present. Further, when Children's Advocates goals are thwarted by the need for cooperation and contribution from a particular group or discipline, we actively encourage membership which will be beneficial toward those goals. Growth in keeping pace with the capacities of the organization is essential. Too rapid growth in numbers affects the communication capabilities of the group; it could hamper smooth progress.

When the organization was about two years old, the membership decided to seek incorporation as a nonprofit group in order to be able to accept funds to promote its work. At that time, we made the choice to work toward coordination of services, communication, and education as the areas in which, with our expertise, we could make the greatest impact.

Children's Advocates requires that each delegate (each agency is represented by one or two delegates) contribute two hours weekly to the organization's work. General membership elects officers (president, vice president, recording and corresponding secretaries, and treasurer) who, with the committee chairmen, make up the board which provides the necessary leadership for the organization.

The monthly meetings of the group are a place where differing opinions and attitudes are expressed and where we learn to view a problem from more than one perspective. The group becomes a sounding board for new ideas and proposals.

Although the program for the general membership frequently highlights an existing service or proposal, other programs consist of a member agency simply describing an existing problem—such as the lack of resources in a given area—and asking for group suggestions. As the group has grown and programs have developed, greater opportunity has arisen to utilize the expertise and willing hands of volunteer groups, whose contributions have been invaluable.

In summary, Children's Advocates grew and developed out of a need to turn an individual sense of frustration and helplessness into a feeling of positive direction and achievement in an area with many unmet needs. In the process, feelings are understood and handled, energies are renewed as group members work together, and attitudes change. Programs are developed and, most importantly, the end result is improved services to the neediest of children and families.

A

DE